## DATE DUE

| | | | |
|---|---|---|---|
| JAN 1 9 2000 | | | |
| MAR 1 0 2001 | | | |
| | NOV 1 4 2003 | | |
| | | | |
| | | | |
| | | | |
| | | | |
| | | | |
| | | | |
| | | | |
| | | | |
| | | | |
| | | | |
| | | | |
| | | | |
| | | | |

# Irish Glass

FABER MONOGRAPHS ON GLASS
edited by R. J. Charleston
★
NINETEENTH CENTURY BRITISH GLASS
*Hugh Wakefield*

MODERN GLASS
*Ada Polak*

SPANISH GLASS
*Alice Wilson Frothingham*

IRISH GLASS
*Phelps Warren*

A. Oval bowl on separate stand. Height 17⅞ in.; length of bowl 15⅛ in. Late eighteenth century. Probably Cork. Collection, The Marquess of Bute. (See page 91)

# Irish Glass

## *The Age of Exuberance*

PHELPS WARREN

Charles Scribner's Sons
New York

748,2

Warren

725187

A-3-71 (I)

Printed in Great Britain

Library of Congress Catalog Card Number 72–152561

SBN 684–12426–2

For
**S T L C**

# Contents

# Contents

# Contents

# Plates

## Plates

# Foreword

'Irish glass' has long been a phrase to conjure with in the world of antiques, and more 'Waterford glass' has been sold than was ever produced, during the active lifetime of the Waterford factory, by all the glasshouses of the island combined. Yet the criteria by which a glass may be judged as of Irish origin are by no means simple, and half the confident judgments advanced on 'Irish glass' have no basis in fact whatever. The first steps in an advance towards greater knowledge and more reliable judgment were taken by the late M. S. D. Westropp in his classic work *Irish Glass*, published in 1920. This book, however, dealt with the whole known history of its subject back to the seventeenth century, and had proportionately less space and fewer illustrations to devote to the 'Anglo-Irish' period of the late eighteenth and early nineteenth century, when owing to economic and political circumstances English glassmakers migrated to Ireland and the transplanted industry acquired an Irish accent. Mr. Warren has concentrated his study on this important but difficult period, and by gathering together almost every important glass with a documentary claim to being of Irish origin, has firm ground under his feet when proceeding to analyse the Irishness of Irish glass. Himself a collector, he enlivens his careful treatment of the facts with a palpable enthusiasm.

R. J. CHARLESTON

# Acknowledgements

It would be difficult if not impossible to name individually all the museum curators and glass collectors who have generously given help during the years spent in assembling material for this book. Insofar as photographs alone are concerned, acknowledgement of their sources has been made under each illustration, and it is a grateful task to give thanks to the personnel of the institutions and to the private collectors named, without whose co-operation and good will the pictures could not have been assembled.

In addition, for the privilege of showing examples from the Down Hunt Club glass collection I am indebted to Colonel M. C. Perceval-Price; also to the Cork Vocational Education Committee for courtesy in permitting use of photographs of glass belonging to the Crawford Municipal School of Art. Thanks are due to the Cambridge University Press for permitting the quotation in Appendix C; and acknowledgement is made to the Trustees and Director of the Wadsworth Atheneum, Hartford (Connecticut), for permission to use material in an article of my authorship published in its *Bulletin*. The staff of the National Library of Ireland gave me imaginative help in my research in its Irish newspaper files.

Also, for extending help in many different ways, I am grateful to the following: the Marquess of Bute for permitting use of material in his archives, and to Miss Catherine M. Armet, who extracted from the archives much of the material in Appendix G; RADM Ernest M. Eller, USN(Ret.) for material from the United States Navy Department archives pertaining to Captain Isaac Hull; Wilfred A. Seaby, Director of the Ulster Museum, Belfast; the Honorable Desmond Guinness, President of the Irish Georgian Society, and Mrs. Guinness; Mr. Percy LeClerc, State Inspector of Public Monuments, Dublin; Mrs. R. G. Miller of Dublin and the Reverend R. M. L. Westropp of Windermere, children of the late M. S. Dudley Westropp; and Sir Anthony Weldon, Bart., of County Donegal. In the forming of my own collection I am grateful for the advice over the years of Mr. Howard Phillips, Mr. Derek Davis, and, for his very special help, I extend thanks to Mr. Martin C. F. Mortimer of Delomosne & Son Limited, London.

Throughout the preparation of this book, Robert J. Charleston,

## Acknowledgements

Editor of the Monographs on Glass, has been encouraging and patient, generous with his knowledge and counsel, always helpful in his criticism. My greatest debt is to him.

PHELPS WARREN

*New York*

# Introduction

Our concern in this study is with glass made in Ireland at the close of the eighteenth and the beginning of the nineteenth centuries.

In the agelong history of glass, a significant moment occurred in Ireland during a fifty-year period from 1780 until about 1835. Irish glass prior to 1780 was indistinguishable from glass made in England. After 1780 glass made in Ireland responded to changing conditions and a unique Irish glass style was developed. This period of the Anglo-Irish Revival has been dubbed 'the age of exuberance', with specific reference to the later style of glass cutting. Subsequent to about 1835, the exuberant Irish glass was widely copied and the Irish style ceased to be unique. It is the purpose of this study to recount why that significant moment in glass history occurred in Ireland between 1780 and 1835 and to describe the glass made during it.

Thanks to the early similarity between glass made in England and in Ireland, Irish glass in its maturity has generally been dismissed as 'merely the last phase of English glass making'.[1] It has habitually been relegated to a last chapter or two, with a minimum of illustrations, in studies of English glass invariably written by English authors. With one notable exception there has been no major published work on the subject of Irish glass to help collectors and curators to recognize it and label it accurately.[2] The reputation of Irish glass has increased over the years in disproportion to available information about it. It is these considerations which have led to the present study.

Most books on English glass, with their limited treatment of glass in Ireland, imply that Irish glass is the end of a style and period. In this study Irish glass is viewed as the essential hyphen between late-eighteenth-century glass, and later glass in the international style made in England, on the Continent, and in the New World.

This view is supported in an unbiased over-all history of glass from which we take the following quotation: 'When Irish flat cutting came in, the Dutch did it equally well on a tinted soda glass which could, and does, easily pass for . . . Waterford.'[3] And again, writing of glass makers in the early years of the nineteenth century in numerous European

[1] Thorpe, p. 253.
[2] The exception is Westropp's *Irish Glass*, 1920, long since out of print.
[3] Haynes, p. 133.

countries, another author has said that 'ils façonnèrent et décorèrent à la manière des modèles anglais ou irlandais'.[1]

Again, we read '. . . only the most sentimental bias will deny the Irish glass of Bohemia a place beside the work of the Irish factories themselves'.[2]

Finally, turning toward the west and reading of American Blown Three Mold glass of 1820–1830, one notes the following significant passages: 'There is no doubt that it was inspired by the expensive and fashionable imported Irish and English blown glass with wheel-cut designs'; and again, 'The manufacturers of certain patterns could have given it a trade name such as "American Waterford" which would have been appropriate because of the similarity in design to some of the imported Irish and English cut glass.'[3]

A comment bearing on the identification of furniture is valid in relation to the identification of Irish glass:

. . . The daily sight of fine furniture, living with it, using it, and learning to understand all its qualities, gives one a knowledge that no study of it in museums or other people's houses can possibly provide. One becomes on terms of intimacy with it and from that intimacy one develops an instinct which makes one tell at a glance whether other pieces of the period are genuine or not. There is something about the real article that is as unmistakable as the face of an honest man. . . .[4]

The criteria for the determination of the 'real article' in the field of Irish glass are numerous, varied, and, taken separately, each is fallible. Sound attribution can be made only by the application of each of the criteria, insofar as each is applicable, to each piece of glass. The instinct born of intimacy, mentioned in the preceding quotation, can give generous help to support the criteria.

Among the grounds for determining the 'real article' in Irish glass are the following:

*Impressed names:* Some Irish glass houses made it a practice to impress their names, by the use of moulds, on bases of decanters, jugs, finger bowls, and a limited number of other vessels. While the danger exists that old moulds are used today to make 'deceptive reproductions',[5] impressed marks, accepted with caution, provide guide lines for *both*

[1] Chambon, p. 261.    [2] Thorpe, p. 301.    [3] McKearin, p. 240.
[4] *Duncan Phyfe and the Regency Style*, McClelland, New York, 1939. Foreword: 'The Regency Style' by Edward Knoblock.
[5] As long ago as 1950 collectors were specifically cautioned about reproductions from the original *Cork Glass Co.* moulds. *Antiques*, March, 1950, p. 200: article: 'Glass from Ireland' by E. Barrington Haynes.

Irish and factory attribution. This holds true for Cork, Waterford and Belfast. Unfortunately, evidence of impressed vessels of Dublin origin is confined to several moulded dishes (Plate 21B) and a few finger bowls of assumed but not proven Dublin manufacture. This is an anomalous situation for the capital city which boasted a substantial glass house during the 'age of exuberance'.

*Engraved topical inscriptions:* Although glass was frequently engraved elsewhere than at the factory where it was made, topical engravings, accepted with the same caution as impressed names, provide grounds for attribution. Often they include a place name or the name of an organization identified with a particular locale (e.g., 'Waterford Volunteers', Plate 48); such inscriptions are sometimes guide lines for *both* Irish and factory attribution. To illustrate further, one may refer to the *Cork Corporation* mixing glass in Plate 75D. The engraving suggests a Cork origin for the vessel; it also provides a reasonable attribution for an unengraved glass with similar cutting (Plate 72B*b*). Unfortunately it does not reveal a specific glass house; there were two Cork factories as against only one glass house in Waterford.

*Intrinsic design and applied ornamentation:* The last of the Hanover Georges did not die until 1830, only five years before the terminal date of this study; but at the turn of the century, as Prince of Wales, the future George IV simultaneously closed the period of Georgian grace as – no doubt presiding over a splendid table of exuberantly cut glass, and with a bumper of claret in his hand – he inaugurated what today we define as the Regency period. Insofar as glass is concerned, the evolution of forms and decoration from mid- and late-eighteenth-century style to the Regency style occurred during the years of the dominance of the Irish style. Regency forms were heavy and were expressed with a lavish use of metal. This in turn permitted a lavish use of cutting. In Ireland the skills and techniques to meet the demands of Regency taste were developed by nearly two generations of expatriate Englishmen, German immigrants and the nameless Irish craftsmen who trained under them. Weight, scale, ornamentation, in addition to the basic design of an article, must all be considered in judging its Irishness. Among inherent characteristics, also, the colourlessness of the metal plays an important role in attribution of Irish glass, especially of glass possibly from the Waterford factory.

*Pattern drawings:* Drawings of actual patterns used in the factory at Waterford show clearly many of the designs used during the later years of that glass house. In some cases, the drawings are even accompanied with cutting instructions. These designs are among the most reliable of

# Introduction

guide lines to identification and it is the greatest good fortune that they are for Waterford glass.

*Hallmarks and coins:* Irish hallmarks on silver mountings on pieces of glass may be used with caution to establish Irish origin for the glass and perhaps to provide attribution to a particular city. The centrepiece shown in Plate 27B for example, bears a Dublin hallmark for the year 1787. Other signs of Irish origin which occasionally appear are Irish coins enclosed within glass vessels (Plates 24, 25). While such signs may be of whimsical origin and therefore unreliable, when weighed with other clues to attribution they can be helpful in suggesting both date and locale.

*Tradition and provenance:* Used with discretion, tradition and provenance may be accepted as additional clues to attribution. The pitfall where family tradition is concerned is in wanting to believe it to the exclusion of a lively suspicion regarding it. Actually, except for its proclivity to telescope generations, family tradition is inclined to be fairly reliable. In this study we have been at pains to obtain examples not only of glass belonging to collectors of perspicacity but also of glass belonging to descendants of the Penrose family of Waterford and the Westropp family of Cork.

*The 'over-all picture':* Not to be underestimated in the establishment of attribution is the importance of the 'over-all picture'. A detail of design or cutting which is not thought meaningful in a single example takes on importance when found repeated in numerous examples. Thus the seemingly unique design of a candlestick drip pan (Plate 34C), when found repeated on the bowl and cover of an urn (Plate 33), and seen again on the base of a sifter (Plate 80Be), ceases to be an isolated invention of the designer or craftsman and assumes significance as a characteristic or collective peculiarity.

22

# I

# England 1571-1745

## (a) Development of Metal and Style

An account of the later Irish glass industry must be preceded by a comment on the development of English glass, its composition and style. Although the starting date for our study of Irish glass is 1780, it is necessary to drop back several hundred years before we can move forward.

Since our Irish interests are concerned primarily with metal, form, cutting and wheel engraving, comment on English developments will be confined to those subjects.

'. . . the documentary history of English glass begins with a record of one Laurence Vitrearius-*sc*. Laurence the (? window-) glassmaker – coming from Normandy about 1226 . . .'.[1] He received a grant of land. The record thereafter is replete with names indicating immigration of French glass making families, chiefly from Lorraine. Unfortunately 'no existing specimens . . . can be proved to be the work of the Lorrainers'.[2]

A later and more profound Continental influence upon the manufacture of glass in England came by way of Antwerp, the chief glass centre in northern Europe in the mid sixteenth century. It was to that city that itinerant Italian glass men had migrated from near Genoa and from Venice; and it was from the latter city, by way of Antwerp, that Giacomo (or Anglicized, Jacob) Verzelini came to London in 1571.

To Verzelini belongs the distinction of securing 'a royal licence giving him the sole right to make Venice glasses in England for twenty-one years'.[3] The sovereign whose warrant Verzelini obtained was Elizabeth I. The date was 1575.

It is of the first importance to note that Verzelini was licensed to make 'Venice glasses', that is, glass in the thin, fragile, Venetian style. Such glass is listed in the inventory of Elizabeth's father, Henry VIII, as early as 1542. Its effectiveness depended upon the swift manipulation of the molten metal, and 'the inexhaustible fancy of Venetian glass blowers, whose luxurious, breathtakingly light creations kept Venice the leader of

[1] Haynes, p. 142.  [2] Thorpe, p. 60.  [3] Haynes, p. 145.

23

European taste (in glass) for over 200 years'.[1] The term generally applied to glass in the Venetian style is *façon de Venise*.

In 1674, ninety-nine years after Verzelini received his licence, George Ravenscroft (1618–1681), in London, received *his* patent for a 'particular sort of Christalline Glass', the forerunner of flint glass as we know it today. On June 3, 1676, the Company of Glass Sellers for whom Ravenscroft was working, advertised that the defect previously noted in their 'flint glasses (which were formerly observed to crissel and decay) hath been redressed. . .'.[2]

The glass referred to as flint glass took its name from the employment of calcined flints as its siliceous ingredient. Subsequently, when Ravenscroft achieved a glass made with lead oxide as the flux but with sand as the siliceous ingredient, the term flint glass persisted. Today, glass made with a flux of lead oxide is referred to as lead glass *or* flint glass. Hereafter, however, in this study, referring to English-Irish glass, the word lead will be used except in quotation.[3]

The invention and development of lead glass was to influence glass making for years to come, in England, in Ireland, across Europe and in the United States.

'The essential and distinguishing qualities of good Glass [referring to "white crystal Glass-works (product) of England, i.e. flint, glass"] are, its freedom from specks or striae, and its near resemblance to real crystal in its brilliant, pellucid, refractive, and colourless transparancy.'[4] The new material was softer than the age-old soda-lime glass. Haynes refers to it as having 'a softness of look'. It was also a substantial glass, and it had a longer working range than the glass man's previous metal.[5]

Tentatively at first, then with increased assurance, the English glass man carried on the Venetian tradition of design by manipulation: gadrooning, trailing, threading, serpentine elaboration, handles. But while doing so, he was using the 'new', lead metal.

Subsequently, the *façon de Venise* styles slowly began to disappear. It

[1] Hutton, chapter 'Venice and the Venetian Style'.

[2] Buckley (F), *Glass Trade*, p. 36: *State Papers Domestic*, Car. II, 381, No. 244, as quoted by Thorpe, p. 126.

[3] Equally confusing as the words lead and flint is the term crystal. It is said that in the eighteenth and nineteenth centuries, the term *crystal* was applied in France to English lead glass. Today it is most generally used to designate table glass of a very superior colourlessness and brilliance. It will not be used in this study except in quotation.

[4] Pellatt, p. 27.

[5] The working range is that period of time during which the metal remains in a tractable condition, suitable for manipulation.

has been aptly said that with the invention of lead glass a new aesthetic in glass had been created. The native English craftsmen developed their own repertoire of design, exploiting the optical quality of the lead glass in a bewildering variety of bowl and stem shapes. As their virtuosity developed, they made increasingly lavish use of the handsome, heavy and resonant metal.

Then the glass industry in England, having assimilated Venetian influence, having developed its skill with its own English metal and matured to express a uniquely English glass style, was again subjected to the influence of continental craftsmen.

This time the glass technicians who immigrated to England were Germans. These craftsmen were prompted to bring their skills to England for several reasons. The peace in Europe following the Treaty of Utrecht (1713) made for both prosperity and freedom of migration. And there was the promise of a favourable reception in England, due to the presence of a German monarch who, in the person of George I, acceded to the English throne in 1714.

Contemporary advertisements show that the skills of both cutting and engraving were practised in England by German and Bohemian crafts-men soon after George I's accession.

From about 1714 until 1745 (a crucial date for reasons soon to be explained), the English glass technician under the tutelage of his German fellow worker, developed a variety of cutting motifs which were to be further developed across the Irish Sea as the chief means of orna-menting the glass of the age of exuberance. A list of these devices is given in Appendix A; here it is emphasized that glass cutting, the carving of the metal to achieve refraction of light, depends not only upon clear metal but also upon thick metal. Thus in the golden age of glass cutting to come, heavy section in vessels of utmost purity was to be an essential requirement.

The skill in engraving which the German emigré artisans brought with them to England had been used upon comparatively thin vessels. As Bohemian and Silesian glass men, they had worked upon an improved potash metal of particular hardness and clarity, had exercised their 'painstaking industrious ingenuity' and achieved an acknowledged pre-eminence in the 'delicate and intricate engraving so much in vogue in the second quarter of the eighteenth century'.[1] This mastery they now put to use on the sturdy English lead glass vessels, already dis-tinguished in profile and brilliance and having broad plain surfaces to be worked upon.

[1] Haynes, pp. 106–107.

The proficiency of the German artisans was never developed by the English glass men. 'In their actual use of the (engraver's) wheel, the Englishmen were proficient but never masterly. They turned therefore to simple motives in which such skill as they possessed could be used to advantage . . .'.[1] Thus were subsequently developed the freely rendered flowered glasses with naturalistic ornament which later gave way to stereotyped devices of hardly recognizable flowers, variations on the husk motif, etc. This, briefly, is the background of the limited amount of engraving, of generally inferior quality, observed on Irish glass in the age of exuberance.

## (b) The Parliamentary Acts

We may now survey briefly the English legislative measures which exercised so drastic an effect upon Irish glass development.

The Peace of Utrecht of 1713, which had involved so many princes and powers and seemingly settled so many differences, had not, in effect, truly cleared the air. Within a couple of decades England was again at war and in need of revenue to support it. The glass industry paid in part for the support.

In 1745 an Excise Act was imposed by Parliament. It placed a duty of nine shillings and four pence on each hundredweight of glass materials used in England and Scotland. A Second Excise Tax was imposed in 1777; it *doubled* the duty on lead glass. This time the need for revenue was created by the American War of Independence. Further taxes were laid upon the glass industry in 1781 and 1787. 'Between 1745 and 1787 the flint-glass tax had risen from 9s. 4d. to 21s. 5½d. . . . per hundredweight.'[2]

It will require little imagination to relate the effect upon contemporary glass of these taxes *on the weight of the metal used before cutting*. The very nature of the English lead metal dictated sturdy design, great weight and refractive cutting. Because the 1745 Excise and subsequent taxes made weight so costly, the glass cutter was left frustrated at his wheel until 1780, when advantageous conditions for working in heavy metal were created again – this time across the Irish Sea.

In January of 1780 the English Parliament, while continuing to penalize with taxes its domestic glass industry, began to ease the restrictions it had imposed upon Irish industry, including those upon the manufacture of glass. Thus legislation provided the economic reason for

[1] Thorpe, p. 242.    [2] ibid., p. 286.

glass interests to move from England to Ireland. Production of glass increased in Ireland, and this led, in due course, to the stylistic effulgence of the Irish glass of the Age of Exuberance (which at this juncture, as we move on to Ireland, we dignify with capital letters).

# 2

# Ireland 1745 – 1800 – c. 1835

## (a) Style and Function

An advertisement appeared in the *Dublin Journal* in December of 1737 claiming that the wares of the Fleet Street factory in Dublin were ' "for beauty of metal and workmanship equal to those made in London" '.[1] A later advertisement January, 1752, refers to a wide range of glass articles including some with the 'most elegant mounting [*sic*] now used in London'.[2] These advertisements, supported by others in the same vein, strengthen the belief that in glass, as in modes and manners, London set the fashion in eighteenth-century Ireland. Both before and after the 1745 Excise, Ireland was a customer of England. Imported wares traditionally bring with them an especial *cachet*, and there is no reason to suppose the provincial Irish glass man did not emulate the imported article as his facilities and skills permitted.

Since style is so intimately concerned with function, we may appropriately list here the types of vessels and other luxury glass objects which were offered in Irish advertisements in the eighteenth and early nineteenth centuries. The year given after each group represents the year in which the articles were offered. Identical repetitions have been omitted.

'fine large globe lamps for halls, for one to four candles . . . bells and shades, mounted in the newest patterns with brass . . . baskets, sweetmeat, and jelly glasses . . . wine-glasses . . . water-glasses, and saucers . . . dram and whisky glasses' 1746

'water bottles . . . jugs . . . sillybub glasses, sweetmeat glasses for desserts . . . orange glasses, covers for torts, bells and shades; melon-glasses, gardevins' 1746

'water-bottles, claret and Burgundy ditto . . . water glasses with and without feet, and saucers; plain, ribbed and diamond-moulded jelly-

[1] Westropp, M. S. Dudley, R. I. A., *Irish Glass: An Account of Glass-Making in Ireland from the XVI Century to the Present Day*, London, undated (1920), (cited hereafter as Westropp), p. 47,

[2] Westropp, M. S. Dudley, R. I. A., 'Glass-Making in Ireland', *Proceedings of the Royal Irish Academy*, Vol. XXIX, Section C, no. 3, Dublin, 1911, (cited hereafter as Westropp, *Proceedings*), p. 37.

glasses of all sorts and sizes ... comfit ditto ... glass plates for china dishes ... all sorts of cut flowered glasses may be had of any kind to pattern, viz.: wine-glasses with a vine border, toasts, or any other flourish whatsoever; beer ditto, with the same; salts with or without feet ... cruets for silver or other frames, all in squares and diamond-cut; tea-canisters, mustard-pots, crests and coats of arms' 1752

'enamelled, cut, flowered, and plain decanters ... plates, epergnes, and epergne saucers, candlesticks, cans ... cut, flowered and plain salvers ... salts and salt linings, mustard castors' 1772

'carafes, common, dram-, and punch glasses ... goblets' 1781

'tumblers, salad bowls, etc., cut and engraved to the newest patterns ... liqueur, cruet and other stands in silver and plated ware, Grecian and other lamps, lustres and girandoles' 1804–1805

'dessert sets, butter-coolers ... sugar-bowls, cream-ewers ... rummers ... finger-glasses' 1818.[1]

Although by chance not included in the advertisements cited, the following types of vessel or utensil appropriate to the period may also be mentioned: salvers, 'branches of several sorts',[2] ewers, toddy lifters, covered urns, dishes with domed covers, tripod bowls and bowls with turned over rims, kettle drum bowls, ice pails, squares, scent bottles, flasks, hookahs, military services of glass engraved to order or pattern,[3] ship's decanters.

### (b) Taxes, Imports, Exports

'The history of Irish industries in the eighteenth century falls naturally ... into two periods; first, the years 1700–1780, during which the restraints on Irish trade were in full operation, and which may be called the "period of restriction", and second, the years 1780–1800, during which Irish trade was unfettered by any serious restraints and may be called the "period of freedom".'[4] These definitions are apt insofar as the glass industry is concerned.

*The Period of Restriction – to 1780*

The extent of the importation-exportation of glass into and out of

[1] Westropp, *Proceedings*, pp. 36 *et seqq.*

[2] 'Branches' is taken here to mean girandoles or other devices which hold a number of candles.

[3] That is, services for officers' messes or of patriotic organizations. 'Services' are discussed at length in Chapter 9.

[4] O'Brien, George A. T., *The Economic History of Ireland in the 18th Century.* Dublin, 1918, p. 180.

Ireland in the late seventeenth–early eighteenth centuries is debatable. The diverse opinions are very probably academic; what is of major concern and really gives the name to the 'period of restriction' is the Excise Act of 1745.

The duty of nine shillings and four pence per hundredweight, which Parliament levied on materials used in making glass in England and Scotland, was not levied on glass of Irish manufacture. But Ireland was specifically prohibited from all exportation of glass, being prohibited even from competing with the English industry by exporting to England. For thirty-five years she was permitted to supply only her own market, and for even that she had to compete with England, which maintained a monopoly of importation. Incentive for Irish glass houses was thus reduced to a minimum and the ensuing depression in the industry can be measured both by the closing of glass houses which had operated prior to 1745, and 'the success which the industry obtained when it (the 1745 Act) was subsequently repealed . . .'.[1]

*The Period of Freedom, 1780 to 1800; and the Union*

'The Period of Freedom' began when, as noted at the close of the last chapter, Parliament passed into law in 1780 resolutions granting a large measure of free trade to Ireland.

Numerous reasons for Parliament's conciliatory attitude toward Ireland have been found. Among them, of especial interest in connexion with glass, was the organization of the Irish Volunteers, said to have numbered at one time 80,000 men from all over Ireland. This patriot body was dedicated 'to exact Ireland's rights from England and to remain on foot till these were secured'.[2] Its martial enthusiasm is recorded on many pieces of Irish glass, called Volunteer glasses or decanters because they are engraved with mottoes such as 'Success / To / The Waterford Volunteers'.

Following on its initial gesture of conciliation, 'on January 22, 1783, the British Parliament passed an Act renouncing legislative supremacy over Ireland'.[3] 'By a whole system of bounties and preferential duties Irish industries were encouraged and built up against the natural competition of the more highly developed and favoured industries of Great Britain'.[4] Free Trade had come, and for twenty years the 'Period of Freedom' obtained.

[1] ibid., p. 216.
[2] Curtis, Edmund, *A History of Ireland*, Methuen, London, 1964, p. 311.
[3] O'Brien, op. cit. p. 243.          [4] Curtis, op. cit. p. 319.

The grant of Free Trade to Ireland lasted until 1825. In May of 1800 the Union with Great Britain became law by acts of both Parliaments. It proved commercially disastrous to the smaller country. It is said that as early as 1810 it was becoming apparent that Irish prosperity born of the Free Trade of 1780 would suffer. One writer has noted that during the 1785–1792 period Irish export value had increased from £3,779,570 to £5,387,760, or 43 per cent, but during the period 1803–1809 it rose from £5,090,393 to £5,922,591, or only 16 per cent. The reason why we close this study of Irish glass at about the year 1835 is explained in those figures. The Period of Freedom was over.

# 3

# The Glass House Cities and their Factories

During the middle years of the eighteenth century, before Free Trade in 1780, the only Irish city which produced lead glass of a luxury character in significant quantity was Dublin. After 1780 the principal glass house cities were Dublin, Cork, Waterford and Belfast.

All of these cities were located on river harbours already sheltered or capable of improvement, and they were close to the sea. Behind this consistency in their location near navigable water lay the fact that the glass industry had been prohibited the use of wood fuel by Royal Proclamation of James I as early as 1615; glass houses could thus function only either close to collieries or in towns where coal was readily procured. Again, ready access to the sea was of first importance for both the importation of raw materials, particularly of sand, and when exporting was allowed with the coming of Free Trade, for the exportation of finished goods.

We list below, under their respective cities, the glass houses or individual glass men whose names are associated with the industry during the 1780–1835 period.

### (a) Dublin

Eighteenth-century Dublin has been called the 'western Athens'. It was the seat of the British government, a capital city whose splendour is still apparent. The present Bank of Ireland building (1729), built to house the Irish Parliament, Trinity College's library (1712), the Custom House (1781), were public buildings matched in their classic elegance by great private residences such as Leinster House (1745), itself of such a scale that today it serves as the meeting place of the Parliament of Ireland.

In response to its role as a maritime city, Dublin's harbour was improved in 1796 by the opening of its Grand Basin. The construction in 1821 of St. George's Docks, located on the north side of the River

Liffey and east of the Custom House, testifies to the growth and importance of Dublin as Ireland's first port.

At the time when Free Trade was granted, the Dublin glass firm of
greatest consequence was

Richard Williams and Co. 1764–1827 (1829?)
(Also associated with the names of Thomas, William and
Isaac Williams)

This firm's advertisements in the *Dublin Journal* extend over the years;
it is interesting that they also appear in the *Belfast News Letter* and in
the *Limerick Chronicle* as early as 1770.

In 1785, in a petition to Parliament relative to moving Dublin glass
houses outside the city, William and Richard Williams asserted they had
been manufacturing glass in the one place for nearly 30 years and employed about 70 persons.[1] Having started their operations in 1764, only
16 years before Free Trade, the Williams were in a favourable position
when the Period of Freedom began. They survived the Union until 1827.

Indications are that the impetus given to the glass industry by Free
Trade was reflected in Dublin by the starting of only one new factory to
give competition to the entrenched Williams family.

Charles Mulvaney, *et al.*, 1785–1846
(later E. S. Irwin and later still with Charles Irwin)

Charles Mulvaney, who earlier (and later) is found in *Dublin Directories*
as 'merchant', in 1788 asserts he 'manufactures' a wide range of luxury
glass 'from first process to finishing'.[2] He also operated a wholesale and
retail warehouse. Sometime prior to 1788 a firm, Jeudwin, Lunn and Co.,
was associated in Dublin with the manufacture of bottle glass. Later
repetitions of identical addresses for Lunn's enterprises and those of
Mulvaney lead to the thought that Mulvaney had a connexion with Lunn
which made the former a 'manufacturer'. The Mulvaney history is hard
to unravel, what with old partnerships being dissolved, new partnerships
being formed, bankruptcies, moves. It is reasonably clear that Mulvaney
did not retire from the Dublin scene until 1835 and that as co-manu-
facturer (with Lunn) or as a merchant or both, in a career of forty-odd
years he achieved a high place in the industry, usurping the Williams
position. He took E. S. Irwin as partner before his retirement, and E. S.

[1] Westropp, p. 59.    [2] ibid., p. 54.

Irwin in turn was joined by his brother, Charles. But that later history lies beyond our terminal date of about 1835.

## Jeudwin, Lunn and Co.

Although it is uncertain whether this firm did in fact make luxury glass, its name may not be omitted from a Dublin glass house list within our period because of its connexion with Mulvaney noted above. The extent of its operation in 1761–1762 is revealed in a petition wherein they stated they 'employed about sixty workmen of whom about fifty were English; and that they could manufacture about £5000 worth of glass in the year'.[1]

Chebsey, Thomas and John 1786–1787–1798
    (also Peter Chebsey, also John Raper)
Ayckbowm, John Dedereck
    (also J. D. Ayckbowm & Co)
    (also Ayckbowm and Murphy)
Mary Carter & Son
Francis Collins
Armstrong Ormond Quay

The Chebseys were glass manufacturers; they are known to have made plate glass, to have exported lead glass to Cadiz, and to have operated a warehouse where they offered an assortment of what may be interpreted as luxury glass. The exact nature of their operations is obscure, and their existence was of short duration.[2]

Ayckbowm[3] is of interest not as a probable though minor manufacturer in Dublin, but for several other reasons. He was a scion of German émigrés who appear to have specialized in London in both manufacturing and exercising their German skill in glass cutting. It is probable that in Dublin J. D. Ayckbowm cut blanks and operated as a retailer. An advertisement of 1774 in the *Limerick Chronicle* states 'Ayckbowm & Co., Glass Manufacturers from London, are selling cut glass in Limerick for 10 days',[4] and confirms the ubiquitousness of this family in Anglo-Irish glass affairs.

[1] ibid., p. 53.
[2] It is of interest that this comparative newcomer in Dublin obtained in 1788 an order for 'lustres' for St. Patrick's Hall, Dublin Castle, the one-time scene of the investiture of the Knights of St. Patrick. It appears that the order resulted from a visit to the Chebsey premises by the Lord Lieutenant of Ireland and the Marchioness of Rockingham (Westropp, pp. 61 *et seq.*).
[3] Spelled '*Ayckboum*' by some authorities.      [4] Buckley, p. 128.

Mary Carter & Son and Francis Collins are believed to have been merchants only, but mention is made of them because we shall meet with them again in a later chapter. Although listed in *Dublin Directories*, no advertisements of Mary Carter's are known; Francis Collins, also listed in *Dublin Directories*, is cited in one advertisement only and that implies a retail activity.

## (b) Belfast

Belfast is situated on the river Lagan which debouches into Belfast Lough, an estuary of the North Channel penetrating deeply into Ireland's north-east coast. This combination of river and Lough has given Belfast a splendid harbour which early made the city a centre of the linen industry (see Plates 37A, B), and of shipbuilding.

Glass making in Belfast may be said to have begun just prior to the Period of Freedom and the beginning of Free Trade.

Benjamin Edwards, Senior 1776–1812
(Members of the Edwards family carry on manufacturing and warehousing operations until 1870)

Benjamin Edwards' career had started in Bristol, England. About 1771 he migrated to a town called Drumrea near Dungannon in Co. Tyrone, fifty miles from Belfast, where there were collieries. Advertisements of 1772, in both the *Dublin Journal* and *Belfast News Letter*, indicate that the factory of which he was apparently superintendent offered the usual wide range of luxury glass. The following year, however, this enterprise was advertised to let, and Benjamin Edwards is next encountered in Belfast in 1776.

There, at the Ballymacarrett (East) end of the Long Bridge, he erected a glass house and resumed a career which lasted until 1812, when he died (although he had in point of fact 'retired' in 1811). The earliest advertisement of Edwards to come to light is in the *Belfast News Letter* dated 'From FRIDAY January 12, to TUESDAY January 16, 1781.' Specifically dated 'Belfast Jan. 8th, 1781,' the notice reads, in part: 'BENJAMIN EDWARDS, at his FLINT GLASS-WORKS in Belfast, has now made, and is constantly making all Kinds of enamel'd cut, and plain Wine Glasses. . .'.

He also fathered three sons, John, Hugh and Benjamin, Junior, and he had acquired, in addition, a son-in-law, William Ankatell. These he instructed in glass making, and subsequently he took them into partnership (1800).

The Edwards record thereafter is so full of the dissolving of partnerships, reorganizations of companies, openings, closings, bankruptcies, on the parts of these five men that it makes a long, dull and necessarily incomplete story. A few names associated with their careers should be mentioned, however, and the fact that Edwards, Senior, this former Bristol manager-craftsman, advertised in 1781 that he had brought a glass cutter from England 'who was constantly employed'[1] should not be overlooked.

Newry is a small town some forty miles south of Belfast, connected with the sea by an eighteenth-century canal and the Carlingford Lough. It enjoyed, after Free Trade, a small, somewhat confused position in the Irish glass industry. Short-lived factories did exist there, glass was imported there from Waterford and Cork (possibly blanks for cutting?), Newry glass itself was exported to Dublin and perhaps abroad, and it was sold locally. To this minor centre the Benjamin Edwards and Sons partnership repaired and opened a warehouse in 1800; their partnership was dissolved three years later.

John Edwards, who in 1803 erected a glass house in Belfast, went bankrupt in 1804 and his house was taken over by one Joseph Wright, whose partners were John Martin, John McConnell and George Thompson, whom we shall meet again below.

In 1811 Benjamin Edwards, Senior, let his factory, which was then carried on by a partnership called Chaine and Young.

Benjamin Edwards, Junior, upon his father's death in 1812, intended to carry on the business but by 1815 he had sustained such reverses that in the following year the foundries at Ballymacarrett and Newry were offered for sale. Though the family partnership had been dissolved in 1803, some member of the family must have continued the Newry enterprise until this 1816 transaction.

Not to be downed, Benjamin, Junior, seems to have been back in business in 1824, but not successfully; in 1827 new names appear when T. J. Wright & Co (for Thomas Joseph Wright, Robert and A. J. McCrory) buy out Benjamin, Junior. They in turn dissolved in 1829 and the previously owned Edwards' stock, glass pots, sand and utensils, were sold.

This fragmentary record of the Edwards glass house operation may be summarized thus:

36 years of Benjamin Edwards, Senior's, work – 1776–1812
15 years of Benjamin Edwards, Junior's, work – 1812–1827

[1] Westropp, *Proceedings*, p. 45.

After their partnership with their father was dissolved, or after Benjamin Edwards, Junior's, forced sale in 1816, John and Hugh Edwards were very probably employed by firms succeeding to their family's failing enterprises.

Belfast Glass Works 1803–1840
(Associated name: Geddes, McDowell & Company, which appears to have supplanted the original group of Wright, *et al.*)

When John Edwards, son of Benjamin, Senior, went bankrupt in 1804, a year after erecting his own glass house, it was taken over as we have seen by Messrs. Wright, Martin, McConnell and Thompson. In 1809 this apparently successful group was advertising 'they could supply goods equal, if not superior, to any manufactured in Ireland'. Benjamin Edwards, Junior, and Hugh Edwards, being still in business at this point, and jealous of their years of experience, answered that advertisement with one the following month in which they pointedly referred to 'persons totally unacquainted with the nature of any kind of glass'.[1]

The Belfast Glass Works survived this understandable pique by the Edwards; the latter, as noted, did not survive their competition. The Belfast Glass Works carried on for over thirty years until, upon the death of one of the partners, negotiations for the sale of the assets were begun, in 1838, and in 1840 these were sold to one John Kane (see below, under Wheeler).

Smylie & Co 1786–1800
(Associated names: Dunningham Greg, James T. Kennedy, Charles Brett, Hugh and Robert Hyndman)

This firm is included solely to complete the record; it was variously a bottle glass and window glass factory. It is of interest because in 1824, having long been idle, the ground and glass house thereon were taken over by Benjamin Edwards, Junior.[2]

[1] ibid., p. 47.
[2] It is indicative of the involved merchandizing methods of the period that Smylie & Co. appear also to have had Dublin interests, having listings in directories there from 1800 to 1820 though referred to, even in those years, as 'Belfast Glass Merchants' (Westropp, p. 109). It may have been that although the Smylie company had retired from the Belfast manufacturing scene, it retained an interest in a surviving glass house there and was acting in Dublin as an outlet.

John Wheeler 1823–1825
(Associated names: J. Stanfield, John Kane)
(New Glass House 1823–1825)
(Shamrock Glass House 1825–1850)

Wheeler had been an Edwards employee. In 1823 he erected his own glass house at the east end of the Long Bridge, accepted partners in 1824, entitled his plant the New Glass House, sustained a fire, then retired (together with J. Stanfield) leaving John Kane alone. Kane in turn carried on, changed the name, and from 1829 until 1850, the Shamrock Glass House offered 'rich cut glass', etc.

### (c) Waterford

Waterford is on the river Suir, close to its confluence with the river Nore, both streams reaching deep into southeastern Ireland. The town itself lies fifteen miles from the open sea; vessels outward bound with their cargoes of glass sailed for two hours down the quiet waters of the harbour till they rounded the promontory of Hook Head and pressed on to open sea.

The Waterford Glass House was founded in 1783; prior to that date no glass appears to have been made in the city since 1740. The Waterford Glass House was the only glass house in the community between 1783 and 1851, the year when it closed for good.[1] It was the product of this single factory which made the name Waterford synonymous with the finest cut glass. In fact, the name Waterford in connexion with luxury glass has ceased to be a noun and has assumed an attributive form as in the case of a 'chippendale chair' or a 'delft plate'.

Because there is only one factory to deal with, the picture of the glass interests of the city of Waterford is far less clouded than is the history of Dublin's or Belfast's interests. And because of the fortunate existence of records pertaining to the single factory, we may examine Ireland's most famous glass house, its history, owners and product, in gratifying detail.

It will be convenient to summarize the history, later filling in the skeleton outline.

**Waterford Glass House 1783-1851**
\*George and William Penrose 1783–1799
  (Associated names: John Hill of Stourbridge, Francis

---

[1] Glass making was resumed in Waterford in 1952.

Penrose, Waterford Flint Glass Manufactory)

*James Ramsey, Jonathan Gatchell, Ambrose Barcroft 1799–1811

*Jonathan Gatchell 1811–1823
    (Associated name: Joshua Gatchell)

*Gatchells & Walpole 1823–1830
    (Associated names: Jonathan, James and Samuel Gatchell, Joseph Walpole, George Gatchell, Elizabeth Walpole, Nathan Gatchell)

*Gatchell, Walpole & Co 1830–1835
    (Associated names: Nehemiah Wright, Gatchells, Walpole and Gatchell, Jonathan Wright, Samuel Miller)

*George Gatchell 1848–1851

* The names preceded by asterisks appear to have been the actual proprietors for the years shown; the name Waterford Glass House remained constant during the several changes of ownership.

The name Penrose is a familiar one in southern Ireland; the 1839 Directory and Almanac Map of Waterford show a Penrose Lane leading to *The Quay* from Anne Street and 'Glassh^e Lane', and in the city of Cork there is still today a Penrose Quay.

The brothers George and William Penrose were Irish men of wealth. They grasped the financial opportunity presented by the simultaneous restriction on glass making in England and the 1780 grant of Free Trade to Ireland. They founded the Waterford Glass House, and they first advertised their company and its glass in the *Dublin Evening Post* of Saturday, October 4, 1783. Under the headline '*Waterford Glass-House*', the advertisement reads:

George and William Penrose having established an extensive Glass Manufactory in this city, their Friends and the Public may be supplied with all Kinds of plain and cut Flint Glass, useful and ornamental: They hope when the Public know the low Terms they will be supplied at, and consider the vast expence attending this weighty undertaking, they will not take offence at their selling for Ready Money only. They are now ready to receive orders, and intend opening their Warehouse the 1st of next month. Wholesale Dealers and Exporters will meet with proper Encouragement.   Sept. 22, 1783.

In preparation for this 'weighty undertaking' and accounting for part of the 'vast expense' was the employment by the Penroses of one John

Hill, a glass maker of Stourbridge, Worcestershire, who assembled for them workmen qualified in all phases of glass making, 'from the mixing room to the cutter's wheel.'[1]

How many men Hill brought with him from England to Waterford is not known. There is, however, a statement in a Petition of George and William Penrose, to be found under the date of January 24, 1786, in the *Irish House of Commons Journal*, to the effect that the glass works employed 'from fifty to seventy manufacturers, who have mostly been brought from England . . .'. There is also a reference to the Irish workmen employed for training.

It is certain that John Hill provided the creative talent for the Penrose plant. Although his stay in Waterford lasted only three years, it was his knowledge of glass chemistry, his standard of quality and his sense of design, imparted in that short length of time, which established the pre-eminence of the Waterford Glass House product.

It is because of this, and because of the human interest which attaches to the severance of his Penrose employment, that the following personal history of Hill is related.

Hill, who is thought to have been a Quaker, had a friend named Jonathan Gatchell, a clerk in the Penrose office, who was a Quaker. In a letter[2] believed to date from 1786 and addressed simply to 'Mr. Gatchell', Hill wrote to his Quaker friend as follows:

Dr Jonothan [*sic*]

It is impossible for me to express the feelings of my poor mind when I acq. thee that I am obliged to leave this Kingdom, my reasons I need not tell thee, but I sincerely wish I had been made acquainted with the base ingratitude of the worst of Villians sooner & probably then I might have remedied it, but now 'tis too late. For heavens sake don't reproach me but put the best construction on my conduct. I wish it was in my power to pay thee & all my Creditors but if ever Fortune should put it in my power depend upon it I will satisfy every one – My mind is so hurt I scarcely know what I write. I sincerely wish thee every success & am tho' the most miserable of mankind

thine very Sincerely

J. Hill

[1] Thorpe, p. 266.
[2] Gatchell Letters, Waterford Glassworks, No. 1–78, 154–1956, Vol. I, document 7(a), National Museum of Ireland.

The significance of the above letter is indicated in the following document:

(*obverse*)

What a world of family incidents grew out of the event about which these letters were wrote – The writer J. Hill was a person in the employment of the Penrose's as a compounder at the Glass House & he alone knew the mixing of the materials – My Uncle Jonathan was a clerk there with Hill, & by these letters it is clear a friendship subsisted between them – Of Hill I know nothing but that he was an Englishman who failed in business – but this is certain he was either innocent or guilty of a crime laid to his charge by the Wife of one of the Penroses (a Nevins) – of his guilt I have heard it doubted & that he felt keenly as an injured man is evident from his letters – He fled over to France & more was not heard of him, except that grateful for my Uncles kindness & pity he gave him his receipt for compounding the Glass – this made my Uncle indespensible to the Penroses & he succeeded them.[1]

(*reverse*)

These notes were written by my Uncle Jonathan Wright nephew of my Grandmother's brother Jonathan Gatchell

Sam H. Wright[2]

These involved family relationships may be explained as follows: Jonathan Gatchell, the recipient of John Hill's bounty, had a nephew named Jonathan Wright, author of the long explanatory note. He in turn had a nephew named Samuel H. Wright who made the note on the reverse of the original document. The introduction of the Wright family into these affairs, which have already embraced the Penrose and Gatchell families, will be explained below. It is important to realize the involvement of these families because of the number of pieces of glass associated with them shown in the plates.

The longhand 'receipt for compounding the Glass', referred to in Jonathan Wright's explanation, will be found in Appendix D. The writing is believed to be Gatchell's; the information was probably given to Gatchell orally by John Hill.

[1] ibid., 7(b).
[2] Beneath Wright's signature is the date of December 17, 1917, in a hand presumed to be that of M. S. Dudley Westropp, the date being the approximate time when he had received these invaluable documents from Mr. Wright himself.

Jonathan Gatchell (1752–1823) was thus precipitated in 1786, at the age of thirty-four, into a key position with the Waterford Glass House. That, possessed of his important secrets, he had come to terms with the Penroses is attested by a letter to him from his brother Joshua in Dublin. Under date of June 10, 1786, Joshua writes: 'I received thine of 24 ulto, and I am very much pleased to hear of thy agreement with William Penrose. . . .'[1]

From 1786 until 1799 Jonathan patiently learned the business and bided his time, though doubtless his position in the glass house was immeasurably improved. In 1799, one Penrose brother having died, Jonathan acquired two partners and bought out the remaining Penrose brother. A dozen years later he owned the entire business and thereafter remained proprietor until his death in 1823. His six-page will dated the '30th day 3rd mo year 1823', identifying him as 'Jonathan Gatchell of the city of Waterford glass manufacturer',[2] clearly establishes him as a man of substance and a citizen of stature in his community.

What is important in this success story is that through the Period of Freedom from 1783 until the Union of 1800, and subsequently for two decades, the standards of quality established by Hill, and the techniques by which that quality was obtained, which were Hill's legacy to Gatchell, remained with the Waterford Glass Works.

Jonathan Gatchell had numerous brothers and two sisters. Of the latter, Susannah Gatchell married Nehemiah Wright and Sarah Gatchell married William Walpole. The sons of the Gatchell–Wright union, Jonathan, John and Nathan, appear from the surviving correspondence to have been the executive heads of the business, with Jonathan as the most active of the three. Of the Gatchell–Walpole union there was a son, Joseph, who died in 1824. The Elizabeth (Betsy) Walpole who figures largely in the correspondence, signing herself in letters to Jonathan Wright as his 'affectionate cousin', was heiress of Joseph's interest in the glass house.

Jonathan and John Wright were frequent correspondents with their father Nehemiah in Dublin, with their brother Nathan and with each other. Betsy Walpole's letters are directed chiefly to Jonathan Wright.

While frequently spaced widely apart in point of time, and generally one-sided, this correspondence contains much valuable information about the later period of the Waterford Glass House operations.

Thus, for example, we observe the 'formation of the New Company of

---

[1] Gatchell letters, etc., document 8.
[2] Gatchell letters, etc., document 18(c).

Gatchells and Walpole', described in a letter to Jonathan from John Wright dated Waterford '1 [?] of 6th month 1823'. The 'New Company' was to consist 'of my uncles Jonathan Samuel and James and Joseph Walpole . . . this relates to the Glass Works only, the retail Ware room on the Quay (which is my department) & the stock on hand there he (i.e., probably Jonathan Gatchell) reserves entirely to himself and of course it now becomes a separate establishment quite distinct from the Glass House and is to be supplied with glassware by the company like any other Customer. This reservation my uncle no doubt has made for the purpose of leaving to my Aunt . . .'.[1]

A few years earlier, in 1819, apropos of his outstanding accounts overseas, Jonathan writes to 'Dear Brother' that one of his accounts 'gives me no hope of anything soon' and complains of 'about £1100 unsettled in Philadelphia £60 in N. York £300 in Halifax nearly £600 in Nf Land and £150 in Quebec'.[2]

From Waterford, 10 years later, the '12th month 14th day 1829', John Wright tells 'Dear Nathan': '. . . I wish I could give as favorable an account of our business here but am sorry to say the reverse is the case, the Glass Business I believe never was in so deplorable a state as it is at present – the Glass Houses in the North and in Dublin are selling at prices so ruinously low as never could be afforded were they paying the Excise Duty fairly, and should this system continue, the fair Manufacturers cannot expect to compete with those who have no scruples to restrain them from smuggling; this in addition to the general depression of the times makes business at the Glass House extremely bad . . .'.[3]

Contrasting with that gloomy report, we get a pretty picture of a retail glass shop situated on the river Suir when, in 1830, Jonathan Wright tells his father 'the alteration is now nearly complete on the Quay and they have the finest shop in Waterford – a door in the center & two windows 10 feet in length . . .'.[4]

In a letter mixing pleasant pursuits with business, Jonathan Wright tells his brother Nathan (1831) about a book sale when 'G. Gatchell had bt 12 vols & 1 book of Plates of Froissarts Chronicles which he'd be willing to sell for 3£ . . . excepting the interest I may take in such matters as books I have not much here.' Referring to business in the same epistle, he tells of a venture: '. . . Geo Saunders and Geo G(atchell) will start for Swansea with a venture of cut Glass which it is our anxious

[1] Gatchell letters, etc., document 18(a).
[2] Gatchell letters, etc., document 17.
[3] Gatchell letters, etc., document 29.
[4] Gatchell letters, etc., document 41.

wish to keep down in Stock – our plain goods we sell as fast nearly as they are made'.[1]

But by 1832 Jonathan Wright in Waterford begins to feel a competition which the Glass House had not previously experienced and under date of '5th of 4th of 1832' he consults his father Nehemiah in Dublin: 'We are now about closing our Spring Shipments which have been small this year decreasing I believe from our rivals the Scotch and English manufacturers lowering their prices for foreign trade while we have lowered ours only for our home market – t'is true the home trade is attended with less risque and brings a quicker return but we have still some regular and punctual correspondents whom it would be well to retain – which can only be done by revision of our prices for Export – this we cannot do but by a comparison with the prices of others . . .' and he goes on to ask his father to make inquiries in Glasgow for a 'List of the Export Prices of Flint Glass principals (sic.) such articles as would suit the Newfound (sic.) trade . . .'. Also, he says 'The same would be very desirable from Edinburgh & Newcastle'.[2]

Meanwhile, partner Elizabeth Walpole is observed undertaking to do her share of marketing Waterford glass. Writing to Jonathan from Exeter in November 1832, she explains her anxiety to sell to a local firm called Eardley's, and to open an account for the Waterford Glass House in Plymouth. She asks to be sent '2 or 3 pair of "rich cut" decanters, 2 or three pr of kniferesters, a dozen of reflecting tumblers, a few sugars all richly cut in different style and of different patterns . . .'.[3]

In a rare instance of consecutive and related correspondence, we have two further letters relating to Eardley's. In March, 1833, Jonathan writes to Elizabeth Walpole: 'E. Eardley's Glass has been forwarded . . . and we have had directions to repeat the same order next month . . .',[4] while from Exeter in April, 1833, Elizabeth Walpole tells Jonathan in Waterford: 'I called on E. Eardley last week, he seems in good spirits about his connection with us, was in expectation of hearing from thee respecting phials and confectioners he wishes to know if we can undersell the English manufacturers in these articles. I hope we can as it undoubtedly is a great trade in this country.'[5]

But Elizabeth's mind was not alone upon selling. Apparently the Glass House had installed, or was planning to install, steam power sometime prior to December of 1832, for on the sixth of that month she

[1] Gatchell letters, etc., document 48.
[2] Gatchell letters, etc., document 52.
[3] Gatchell letters, etc., document 65.
[4] Gatchell letters, etc., document 72.
[5] Gatchell letters, etc., document 73.

writes from Exeter very firmly, to Jonathan in Waterford: 'If the engine pour in such a flood of goods as that there is no room, and that sales cannot be effected in self defense, it would seem desirable that the engine should be stopped, but why with this in view incur the expense of a boiler £32: if the cutting is to be done by hand in future, at least while the present partnership lasts, is it not a useless expenditure to my Uncle Nathan and to me to have a boiler put up for which no allowance will be made to us on our retirement?'[1]

While Jonathan and John Gatchell and their cousin Elizabeth Walpole were thus dealing with the routine and extraordinary problems of running the glass house and selling its product, another member of the Gatchell family was also present although not so prominently identified with the administration.

Thus we read that George Gatchell, Jonathan Gatchell's son, is a 'nice lad' in John Wright's opinion, and, in 1829, is 'employed by me in the Ware room'.[2] This George would appear to be the same person as the purchaser of Froissart's *Chronicles* and the same who went with George Saunders to Swansea on a venture.

Eventually, however, the partnership referred to by Elizabeth Walpole in her letter of December, 1832, was dissolved. The *Dublin Gazette* of Thursday, October 15, 1835, published a notice of 'Dissolution of Partnership' which had linked together several generations of several families since old Jonathan Gatchell died in 1823. The 'nice lad', George Gatchell, now emerges as the individual in control, with George Saunders as his associate; and the glass house continued in operation (until 1851), well past the terminal date of our study. During the last three years George Gatchell was the sole owner.

No history of the Waterford Glass House may omit a special mention of Samuel Miller. His role was a minor one but had he not played it, our knowledge of Waterford glass would indeed be impoverished.

In about 1830, Miller had been a foreman glass cutter in Waterford. From that employment he retained numerous sheets and parts of sheets of drawings of Waterford glass patterns (Plates 95–103). These drawings with their accompanying longhand annotations provide a unique and indispensible guide to the styles in vogue between the years 1820 and 1830.[3]

[1] Gatchell letters, etc., document 69.
[2] Gatchell letters, etc., document 29.
[3] The drawings came into the possession of M. S. Dudley Westropp and are today in the collection of the National Museum of Ireland.

*On the Quality and Colour of Waterford Glass*

There is copious evidence that the Waterford Glass House took particular pains to obtain an absolutely white and colourless glass, and also took pride in the achievement of it. 'In 1813, Carey and Co., china and glass merchants, Cork, advertise that they sell Waterford glass, and state that it is superior to that of any other factory in Ireland. In one of the Waterford letters it is stated that it is regretted that glass ordered could not be sent immediately as the colour was not up to the usual standard ...'.[1]

Again, Elizabeth Walpole takes up the challenge of her potential customer Eardley, in Exeter, and sends for Waterford glass examples 'that he might see for himself' with regard to their freedom from colour.[2]

Ravenscroft made England the richer in 1675-6 by the development of the 'brilliant, pellucid, refractive, and colorless transparency' of lead metal (Pellatt). A hundred years later, John Hill from Stourbridge made Waterford the richer by his knowledge, skill and feeling for the quality of metal, all of which he transmitted to Jonathan Gatchell. In turn, 'For the Gatchells it was a purpose in life to keep their metal clear, their shapes marketable, their cutting clean and exact. . . .'[3]

The famed blue tint, which in many quarters is considered an indisputable sign of authentic Waterford glass, is definitely *not* such a sign. Because the notion is so widespread and so wrong, it is suitable here to relate its origin and a few particulars regarding it.

'There is no information that the glass made at Dublin or Cork had any special characteristics of metal or form . . . but Waterford glass is usually to be distinguished by its pale blue tinge'.[4] With this innocent-seeming phrase, published in 1897, the writer set abroad an opinion which has divided and misinformed students, collectors, curators in museums, dealers and the general public for more than half a century.

It is not that authorities have neglected the attempt to correct the mistaken notion.

In his book published in 1920 Westropp wrote: '. . . it is apparent that the blue tint is not a peculiarity of Waterford glass. As far as I can judge from examining many authentic pieces, the metal of Waterford glass is much whiter than that of any other of the old Irish glasshouses.'

---

[1] Westropp, p. 162.
[2] Gatchell letters, etc., document 69.
[3] Thorpe, p. 275.
[4] Hartshorne, Vol. 2, pp. 366–377. It is interesting to note that Thorpe states in his Bibliography: 'Many of Hartshorne's conclusions have since been superseded,' while at the same time commenting on a 'remarkable book . . . a tribute to the solid methods of the Victorian antiquary' (p. 341).

Subsequently he affirms: 'I have never seen a marked Waterford piece with the blue tint'.[1]

Thorpe, in his work of 1929, surveys the evidence on the subject of the blue tint and affirms 'the metal of Waterford glass is extremely clear and white in color. . . . There is evidence . . . that the firm were at special pains to secure a good, clear white metal.'[2]

In 1952 an exhibition of Waterford glass was held in the City Hall, Waterford, under the auspices of The Old Waterford Society.[3] In his foreword to the catalogue of the exhibit, one of the Society's officers, J. J. Hughes, wrote: 'The statement that Waterford Glass has a distinct bluish tinge has been disproved by experts. Waterford Glass . . . has many . . . qualities, but a bluish color is not amongst them.'

Irish glass with a blue tint does exist, as well as glass slightly yellow and glass tending in colour toward grey, all of which was no doubt intended to be brilliantly white. At this juncture the reader will find it illuminating to glance at the 'Receipts for Making Flint, Enamel, blue & Best Green Glass', Appendix D, and note with what lack of precision they are expressed. The procedure is obviously one of try and try again: 'You will see by the proofs Taken . . . if to high Coloured use a little Arsenick – if to low add more Magneze,' etc.

The blue tint notion may well have been kept alive by the production on the continent of glass cut in what is thought to be a Waterford style. These imitative pieces fall short in several particulars of the originals they presume to match: their rims do not bear resemblance to Waterford glass rims and their shapes are not typical of Waterford shapes. They are markedly blue in colour and the colour is inclined to a uniformity which betrays at a glance a mischievous purpose. The thought persists that the blue tint is an intentional lure to the would-be purchaser of an 'authentic' Waterford article.

### (d) Cork

In describing the site of the city of Cork it seems obligatory among writers to quote Edmund Spenser: Cork stands on 'the spreading Lee that, like an Island fayre, Encloseth Corke with his devided flood' [*sic*].[4]

Below this island city stretches the Lough Mahon, a landlocked harbour sheltered from the sea by a curved channel two miles long. This

[1] Westropp, p. 161.
[2] Thorpe, p. 277.
[3] The event coincided with the resumption of glass making in Waterford by the firm of Waterford Glass Limited.
[4] *The Works of Edmund Spenser*, Macmillan & Co., Ltd., 1929. 'The Færie Queen', IV, XI, 44, 3.

anchorage, called the Cove of Cork, could contain, it is said, 'from four to five hundred sail of merchantmen . . . waiting convoy'.[1] It has been called the last rendezvous for fleets destined for America and the West Indies, but the Custom House records indicate that vessels from Cork did not turn to the west to the exclusion of trade in Denmark, Portugal, Spain and destinations vaguely referred to as 'Africa'[2] and 'Straits'.[3]

Cork was not a glass house city until, in 1783, under the stimulus of Free Trade, local capitalists financed a glass factory just as the Penrose brothers were doing in Waterford in the same year.

In 1783 Messrs Hayes, Burnett and Rowe asked aid of Parliament, saying they had embarked on the undertaking 'by sending a proper Person to *England* to take Plans of the most complete and extensive Works of that Kind (glass houses) . . . as also to employ experienced hands and procure the best Materials . . . they have surmounted all these Difficulties, having procured the most ample set of Materials and Implements, & with a Set of the most able Artificers *England* could afford, . . . they have now erected . . . two Houses, the one for making Bottle and Window-Glass, and the other for Plate and Flint Glass of all Denominations, which are allowed . . . to be as good as any in Europe . . . the Establishment of this great Undertaking has already been attended with an Expence amounting to upwards of 5000 £ . . .'.[4]

Seven months later, using the headline 'CORK GLASS-HOUSES', 'THOMAS BURNETT and Glass House Company' employ the columns of *The Hibernian Chronicle* for Thursday, May 13, 1784, to inform 'the Public, that they have now ready for sale . . . a great Variety of plain, cut, and flint Glass . . .'.

The continuing name for this, the earliest of post-Free Trade glass houses founded in Cork, was the

### Cork Glass Co. 1783-1818
Associated names: Atwell Haynes, Thomas Burnett, Francis Richard Rowe, original partners, doing business as
*Thomas Burnett and Glass House Company 1783–1785
Associated names: John Bellesaigne, Cork Glass-house; Rowe withdraws, 1785, Burnett withdraws, 1787

[1] Marmion, Anthony, *The Ancient and Modern History of the Maritime Ports of Ireland*. London, 1860, p. 521.

[2] Westropp, p. 149; also p. 151.

[3] ibid., pp. 151 *et seqq.*

[4] *The Journals of the House of Commons of the Kingdom of Ireland*, from the Fourteenth Day of October, 1783, Inclusive, to the Seventh Day of September, 1785, Inclusive, in the Reign of His Majesty King George the Third, p. 75.

*Atwell Hayes and Co 1787 –
    Philip Allen becomes a partner of Hayes, a temporary
    closure occurs, then
*Atwell Hayes and William Allen 1792–1793
    a partner named Hickman joins
*Allen, Hickman and Hayes 1793 –
    New Cork Glass House name appears
*Atwell Hayes & Co – *c.* 1800
*Joseph Graham and Co. *c.* 1800–1804
    Associated names William Kellock, Joseph Salkeld
    1804 partnership dissolves
*Joseph Graham and Co 1804–1810
*Smith, White & Co 1810–1812
    1812 White probably retires
*William Smith & Co. 1812–1818

The owners of the *Cork Glass Co.* are shown with an asterisk; it is impossible always to give exact dates except for the opening and final closing date of 1783–1818.

Thus came into being a glass house which was second only to the Waterford glass house in the quality and the individuality of its product. The period of operation of the *Cork Glass Co.* was shorter by far than Waterford's; it did not survive to participate in the exuberance dictated by taste in the 1820's and 1830's as did the Waterford company.

Despite the marked decrease in export business in the years following the Union of 1800, noted in a previous chapter, and a general lowering in the prosperity level which became apparent as early as 1810, two more glass houses opened in Cork; one three years before the closing of the *Cork Glass Co.*, and the other the same year, 1818, in which the *Cork Glass Co.* shut down.

The first one was erected in 1815, the year of the Battle of Waterloo, and was called

**Waterloo Glass House Company 1815–1835**
*Daniel Foley, proprietor 1815–1825
    (Geoffrey O'Connell becomes partner 1825)
*Foley & O'Connell 1825–1830
    (Foley retires 1830)
*Geoffrey O'Connell 're-establishes' 1831–1833
    (O'Connell retires 1833)
*Geoffrey O'Connell 're-commences' 1834–1835
    (O'Connell goes bankrupt)

*The Overseer*, a Cork publication, of Friday, December 13, 1816, relates that Dan Foley's company 'which is now at work' was 'giving employment to more than a hundred persons'. It was predicted by *The Overseer*'s editor that Mr. Foley's glass house would 'shortly' produce 'the most beautiful glass . . . to *dazzle* the eyes of the public and out-shine any competitor'. The self-styled, 'hair-brained itinerant' editor's description of Foley's Christmas treat to his men of a 'whole roasted ox' and of the company's 'band of *glass* instruments' and 'glass pleasure boat and cot', are contained in the same issue.

In 1832, two years after Foley's retirement, his former partner, O'Connell, advertised that upon his re-establishment of the Waterloo Glass works he had restored employment to 100 families,[1] but in 1835 he went bankrupt for non-payment of excise duties.[2] Among his assets to be sold at auction were 'moulds and working implements, together with a steam engine and the fittings-up of the cutting shop; ten excellent pots . . . etc.'.[3]

When the illustrations of impressed examples of this glass house are studied, its 'composite' style will be noted. Its chief characteristic is 'a rope of looped and knotted ribbon-work clumsily engraved round the middle of the body' (of decanters).[4]

A contemporary competitor to the Waterloo Company was the third Cork glass house called the

### Terrace Glass Works 1818–1841
*Edward and Richard Ronayne
  (Associated names: Mr. Norris, a retailer, J. Griffin, manager of the Ronayne's retail shop and formerly of Foley's)
  (1835 they enlarge their premises)
  (1837 they announce new arrangements and repair)
  (1838 their partnership is dissolved)
*Edward Ronayne 1838–1841

The end of the Ronayne story is more interesting than its beginning. In 1841 Edward Ronayne died; at any rate, his name does not occur again and a Joseph Ronayne, together with a Thomas Jones and the Reverend Archibald Robert Hamilton, 'and others', appear to be owners or creditors. Advertised to let in the *Cork Southern Reporter*, September 14, 1841, are 'The old established Terrace Glass Works, Cork . . . Steam engine, tools, and apparatus for turning for forty glass cutters . . . Cork

---

[1] Westropp, p. 123.      [2] Ibid., p. 125.
[3] Ibid.                  [4] Thorpe, p. 281.

is decidedly the best position in the United Kingdom for a glass manu-factory, by reason of its long known character for superior glass, and the vast extent of home trade, and its large exports to foreign markets . . . the small capital necessary to work the concern, and its quick returns, are inducements to capitalists very rarely to be met with.'

Despite the 'inducements', no purchaser came forward to carry on the Terrace Glass Works, and glass making in Cork ceased, nearly 60 years after it had begun.

# 4

# The Extent of the Industry
# and of Its Exports

## (a) The Extent of the Industry

The Irish glass industry within the years 1780 and about 1835 may be expressed conveniently in the following Table.[1]

| Dublin | Richard Williams & Co., 1764–1827 (1829?) |
|---|---|
| | Charles Mulvaney, *et al.*, 1785–1846 |
| **Belfast** | Benjamin Edwards, Senior & Junior, 1776–1827 |
| | Belfast Glass Works, 1803–1840 |
| **Waterford** | Waterford Glass House, 1783–1823 |
| | (Hill and J. Gatchell periods) |
| **Cork** | Cork Glass Co., 1783–1818 |
| | Waterloo Glass House Co., 1815–1835 |
| | Terrace Glass Works, 1818–1841 |

It will be noticed that whereas only two houses opened prior to 1780 and Free Trade (Williams and Edwards), three houses (Mulvaney, Waterford and Cork Glass) opened *after* Free Trade; and that Belfast Glass, Waterloo and Terrace all opened after the Union of 1800, reflecting the prosperity born of Free Trade and the hope of its continuance or increase under the Union.

The contents of the table tally very comfortably with the comment of a writer of 1798.[2] In appraising the Irish glass industry of that time the author wrote: ' "There are five houses now working, two in Dublin, two in Belfast and one in Waterford." ' His references were most probably to Williams and Mulvaney, Edwards and Smylie, and of course to the Penrose factory. A Cork firm was not listed although the Cork Glass Co. was in operation in 1798; possibly it was experiencing one of its recurring closures or a period of uncertain continuation.

---

[1] Discrepancies in dates of factory closings may arise due to the time lag between the actual closing and the newspaper notice of the disssolution of the company or the sale of its assets.

[2] Wallace, *Manufactures of Ireland*, cited by O'Brien, footnote, p. 285.

An earlier writer, Lord Sheffield, in *Observations on the Manufactures, Trade, and Present State of Ireland,* 1785, asserts that ' "nine glass houses have suddenly arisen in Ireland" ',[1] while a later recorder reports glass houses dwindling in number to only three by the time of the Cork Exhibition of 1852.[2]

While there was a continuity of successful management in the records of Williams, and of Waterford (Hill and J. Gatchell period), the records of most of the other glass house operators are replete with dissolutions of partnerships, moves, bankruptcies, changes of function within the industry.

In this connexion it is notable that the *Compendium of Irish Biography,* a tome of 598 pages published in 1878, only 50 years after the close of our period, lists no Benjamin Edwards, no Charles Mulvaney, no 'capitalists' George and William Penrose.

In terms of employment offered, the largest figure we have for the employees of a single plant is Jonathan Gatchell's approximate yearly payroll for the 36 years from 1784 to 1820 of 'nearly two hundred persons'.[3] Most often personnel figures run to 60 to 70 individuals: Gatchell, Walpole & Co. in Waterford in 1832 employed 60 persons; William and Richard Williams in Dublin in 1785 employed 70 people; and in 1761 Jeudwin, Lunn & Co. were the employers of 60 workmen. Ranged against these figures we note that in the year 1800, in Belfast, the linen industry gave employment to 27,000 persons.

In the economic history of Ireland during the Period of Restriction, glass is awarded only a minor mention; the industries of linen, cotton, silk, distilling, pottery and provisioning are all given more attention. Again, in the Period of Freedom, glass manufacture continues to compete for attention with all the industries mentioned, and to them are added the woollen industry, brewing, paper, tanning and shipbuilding.[4]

In view of these considerations, it is obvious that Irish glass manufacture was markedly less extensive than the reputation the product acquired. This is not, however, to denigrate the importance of the glass made during Ireland's 'significant moment' in glass history.

## (b) The Extent of the Exports

The owners or creditors of the deceased Edward Ronayne of Cork referred in their 1841 advertisement to 'the large exports to foreign

---

[1] Westropp, pp. 141 *et seq.*      [2] ibid., p. 142.      [3] ibid., p. 75.
[4] O'Brien, George A. T., *The Economic History of Ireland in the Eighteenth Century.* Dublin, 1918, Chapter XIX.

markets' (Chapter 3, Cork). They are not alone in emphasizing the extent of Ireland's export trade. Westropp quotes opinions from the Sheffield and Wallace books already mentioned. In several instances the opinions refer to export trade to the New World and specifically to New York. In support of these views of early writers, unaccompanied by figures, it is customary to rely on figures published in 1920,[1] extracted from Custom House records.

In the view of the present writer these extracts are misleading. A few examples will show why.

Taking the years 1795, 1796 and 1797, because they are late years in the Period of Freedom, when prosperity was at its height before the post-Union blight set in, we observe the following:

|  | *1795* | *1796* | *1797* |
|---|---|---|---|
| Figures for Dublin exports in 'Drinking glasses' and 'Bottles, dozens' | 131,410 | 191,163 | 403,008 |
| Value of 'other glass ware' | £669 | £925.6.3 | * |
| Of the yearly totals given above for glasses and dozens of bottles, the American states of New York, Virginia and Pennsylvania, and 'New England', received 'Drinking glasses' and 'Bottles, Dozens' as follows: | 112,328 | 153,970 | 396,808 |
|  | *1798* | *1799* | *1800* |
| In the three following years Dublin's drinking glasses and dozens of bottles exported fell to | 25,828 | 22,471 | 16,309 |

It will be noted that 'drinking glasses' are not qualified; we do not know if they are large, small, moulded, blank, engraved, cut, stemmed. We do not know the nature of the 'other glass ware'. We may question the reliability of figures which in two years drop from 403,008 glasses and dozens of bottles to 25,828 (1797–1798), without explanation. Again, we may question these figures because we know that in the years in question there were only two glass houses in Dublin, Williams and Mulvaney; the former (ten years previously) employed 70 persons, while the latter was creating a complicated record of mergers, moves, dissolutions and bankruptcies.

Going a step further to see how these Irish views of exports tally with

[1] Westropp, Chapter VII.

American views of Irish imports during the same period, with specific reference to New York, we turn to a compilation of advertisements and news items garnered from New York newspapers for the years 1777–1799 and 1800–1804.[1]

In the years 1777–1799, only one general entry for imported glass is indexed in the compilation referred to. It is Item 548 and reads as follows:

Edward Massey, Watch and Clock Maker, from Europe, begs to inform his friends and the public, that he has opened his store at No. 113 Pearl-Street near the Old Slip, New York.... He has also for sale 10 hds (i.e., hogsheads) Assorted Glass. *New York Gazette and General Advertiser*, January 8, 1799

No entries are indexed for the 22 year period specifically for Waterford, Cork or Belfast. There are two entries for imports from Dublin: the first (Item 743) refers to a 'crate of hall and stair case bells mounted', and the second (Item 878) refers to books and stationers' supplies.

General Irish glass imports fare better in the years 1800–1804:[2] (Item 301):

Robert Bach. Glass Ware. Ten crates of well assorted IRISH GLASS consisting of decanters, wines, tumblers, cruets, salts, etc. .... *American Citizen and General Advertiser*, August 26, 1801

and again, in the *New York Gazette and General Advertiser*, April 19, 1800, occurs an entry (Item 312) for Irish glass consisting of 'Drams, Wines, Decanters, Goblets, Tumblers, and Pocket Bottles'.

In the four years, 1800–1804, Dublin has no entries, nor Cork nor Belfast; Waterford is represented by an entry for 'lottery tickets'.

While Custom House figures on the quantities of glass exported are thus not reflected in the New York newspaper advertisements, several interesting details relative to the export–import trade with America do emerge from the study of the newspapers.

The first is a reference in the *Commercial Advertiser* of September 22, 1800, to the cargo of the Brig *Zephyr* from Bristol. The vessel brought plated knives and forks, 1300 gross gilt buttons, 200 dozen ivory combs, pocket books, fire irons, etc., *and* glass articles carefully enumerated to the total of 40,240. It is arresting to note that 40,000 glass articles constituted *part* of a brig's cargo.

There are indications that the goods mentioned in New York papers

[1] Gottesman, Ritz Susswein, *The Arts and Crafts in New York 1777–1779*. New York Historical Society, 1954.
[2] ibid., 1800–1804, preface, p. VIII.

were not intended exclusively for the New York market. Expressions 'adapted for New Orleans market', or 'to suit Country Stores', or (for earthenware), '300 crates . . . suitable for this, and the West India market . . . assorted to suit a country store', are frequently to be found in the advertisements.

While we have reservations about the exact terms of reference cited in the Custom House records, there is no reason to question the veracity of the destinations given for the assorted cargoes. These include, of course, numerous port cities on the United States' eastern coast and there are frequent references to the West Indies, Jamaica, Barbados and Antigua. Also appearing on the lists are entries for Canada, Nova Scotia, Quebec, Hudson's Bay. This last listing is for shipments from Waterford which seems to have enjoyed a continuing trade with Newfoundland. Then also we find listed Portugal, France, Spain, Madeira, Denmark, Italy, Jersey and Guernsey, Buenos Ayres, Brazil, Honduras, Surinam, in addition to Africa and the Straits already mentioned.

In summary, the indications are: (1) that the Irish glass export trade was unquestionably widely distributed geographically; (2) because the figures for a cargo ran into the thousands of pieces, figures of total export quantities have very probably been misinterpreted; (3) because Irish glass is popularly identified with 'Waterford', and 'Waterford' is popularly conceived as exuberantly cut luxury glass, wishful thinking has exaggerated the quantity and quality of Irish imports to America.

The bulk of the Irish export product prior to 1790–1800 was of a very utilitarian type of vessel. Drinking glasses and decanters predominated; these were swiftly and inexpensively made by both the better established factories and small fly-by-night glass houses. These small factories, perfectly competent to turn out plain wine glasses and other utilitarian wares, were probably the precursors of the 'smugglers' of whom John Wright complained in 1829. In the New World these useful, non-luxury, articles filled a void which the rising American industry would later supply.[1]

---

[1] ibid., 1779–1799, preface, p. VI:
'. . . The period immediately following the evacuation of the British from New York City presented many problems. . . . The boycott of English goods which preceded and accompanied the Revolution was discontinued, for many advertisements of imports from London suddenly appeared. The newspapers of 1784 and 1785 also carried long lists of goods for sale imported from Paris, Dublin, Liverpool, Amsterdam, etc.' 'However, during the last decade and a half of the eighteenth century, a marked change took place. The craftsman had overcome the initial difficulties of the transition from war to peace and was now in full confidence in his abilities. . . . Less mention (in advertisements) was made of imports and increasing emphasis was placed on American-made goods.'

## The Extent of the Exports

At the turn of the century, and later during the Age of Exuberance, handsome cut glass in limited quantities was exported to the United States. These pieces served as models for the luxury glass referred to as 'American Waterford' in the McKearin quotation in our Introduction. It was not the eighteenth-century exports which gave rise to the Waterford legend in the States but the post-1800 exports of the more choice – and exuberant – Irish product.

Finally, with regard to exports, the idea must be advanced that very possibly more glass stayed in Ireland than is customarily supposed. It is true that in the year 1800 the Anglo-Irish population represented only 10 per cent of the population of Ireland (450,000 of 4,500,000). But in this 10 per cent were the monied and privileged of the country, the persons of taste, fashion and position, the 'home trade' in its 'vast extent' (to use a typical exaggeration of the time) to which the Terrace Glass Works advertisement referred. The great town and country residences like Leinster House, Carton, Powerscourt, the numerous castles and commodious terrace houses which existed along the streets of Dublin and other cities, combined to constitute an avid market; and one continually in need because glass, by its very nature, requires renewal the more it is used – and broken.[1]

One must also remember that glass ware was sold in services. We may recall 'military services of glass engraved to order or pattern', mentioned in Chapter 2. In the Irish glass services shown in our plates there are, even today, approximately 50 pieces in the service of the Corporation of Waterford; approximately 60 pieces in one part of the divided service belonging to the Duke of Wellington; and in the service of the Wadsworth Atheneum, Hartford, Connecticut, there are over 80 pieces representing 14 different types of vessel. We do not know, alas, how many pieces there were in the Waterford service sent in 1788 to Milford and thence to Cheltenham, as mentioned in *The Dublin Chronicle*, but since it was destined 'for their Majesties' use' it may be assumed to have been of notable size.

---

[1] Extracts from *A Frenchman in England*, 1784, in Appendix C, yield interesting details as to the numbers and types of glass vessel required for use at a dinner and during the evening in a country house typical of the Anglo–Irish residences mentioned.

# 5

# On Intrinsic and Applied Characteristics in Glass

## (a) The Intrinsic Characteristics

The development of the metal of which Irish glass was made naturally preceded in our discussion consideration of the characteristics of the glass itself, whether built-in at the time of manufacture or applied after the basic vessel was made.

We propose now to examine the most important of these characteristics, leaving the minor ones for comment when the plates are studied.

It is suitable to start with a tribute to the glass maker written by Apsley Pellatt (1791–1863), the son of a glass man and a glass man himself for many decades.

Perhaps there is no employment so much dependent upon steadiness of nerve, self-possession, and skilful manipulation, as Glassmaking. It requires adroit adaptations of the simplest tools, for the rapid production of manifold forms and designs, upon the most pliant of material, while it retains its heat; and perfection depends not altogether upon long-continued practice, but upon a certain innate tact, without which no workman can ever hope to rise to eminence.[1]

Miss Alice Winchester has written of the 'almost magical quality' of glass, created from the sand of the good earth.[2] The molten sand and its chemical additives, however, await the skill, practice, deftness, teamwork and taste of the glass man, without which it has no more magic than a batch of sluggish metal in a pot.

The glass man, with his 'hot technique' and the aid of his assistants is primarily concerned with characteristics of profile as he shapes a vessel, or as in the case of a tall object such as a candlestick, as he builds it. Of concern also are moulded parts and, of decanters, the neckrings and pouring lips. Starting with a searing, viscous, semi-fluid gather of metal, the glass man creates by manipulation, by adding to the gather, by

---

[1] Pellatt, p. 129.     [2] *Antiques*, June, 1956, Editorial.

shaping it as it cools, and by shearing away excess quantity. This is done according to a pattern usually predetermined. Predetermined also will be whether the vessel is to be engraved or cut, for on this will depend the thickness of the metal of the object the glass man is shaping. The techniques and tools used by glass makers in Irish factories before and during the Age of Exuberance are described and illustrated in Pellatt's *Curiosities of Glass Making* and may profitably be studied by the serious student of Irish glass.

*Profiles of Table Glass Articles*

Decanters: the barrel shaped type of decanter first appears late in the eighteenth century and thus more or less coincidentally with the development of Irish glass subsequent to Free Trade of 1780. It is superseded by the straight sided decanter which is shown in many variations of cutting in the Samuel Miller patterns. (Plates, 95, 96)

Bowls and vases: a turned-over rim and a domed foot are very Irish in character. The latter, it has been remarked, would have been considered a 'needless extravagance' of metal in England in the Excise period, and the same criticism might be applied to the lavish use of metal in the rim, which is prettily turned-over.

Covered bowls and smaller covered jars: the button finial is very characteristic on these. It is appropriate to the flat or gently rounded cover. A pointed finial, sometimes facetted, is likewise appropriate to the aspiring conical cover of the classical urn. Another characteristic of the Irish covered jar is that the cover most frequently sits within an upturned flange of the base, and is not set over or on top of the base.

Kettle drum bowls: the design type of these is shown in numerous styles in the Samuel Miller drawings; the kettle drum bowl is notable for its centred well for the collection of excess juice or dressing.

Plates of varying diameter, also serving plates, and so-called stands used under bowls: a wide, flat flange, which extends horizontally from the cavetto, is characteristic of them.

The ewer, complement of the neo-classic urn in the Age of Exuberance repertoire: it has a pronounced, graceful, high, swan neck handle, which is perhaps more decorative than practical but certainly the former. A pronounced spout, usually almost horizontal, is a characteristic found on Irish vessels of a type between the ewer and the jug.

The jug: a rounded body is characteristic here; the jug has a broad base, is a serviceable, less pretentious article than the ewer.

The serving dish: an oval form is the predominant one; it is remarkable for the number of sizes, identical in shape, in which it is produced, and for the variation in the thickness of the metal used for its sides. This may be observed when the dish is viewed from above, the sides being then visible in section. Occasionally the serving dish is square (Plate 66c); octagonal (Plate 64A, B).

## Moulds

The practice among the Irish glass houses of using fluted metal moulds for the bases of decanters, jugs and finger bowls has already been noted. The gather was blown into the mould and later removed in a semi-soft state for further working. It is suggested that these moulds were probably used for the cheaper vessels[1] but this is perhaps open to question. Impressed examples vary in quality and are certainly not uniformly of poor quality; but unquestionably use of moulds did expedite manufacturing. It is established that some Waterford moulds were obtained from London.[2] On the other hand, Jonathan Wright told his brother Nathan in Dublin, in 1832, '. . . we want the bottle moulds badly from Aldrit.'[3]

But the most significant detail relative to moulds is that in addition to being comb fluted on their sides, which flutes were sometimes carried under and appear on the bases, the moulds frequently bore in intaglio the name of the glass house for which they were made (Plate 16B; this photograph has received no retouching). They thus left the glass house name in relief on the bottom of the vessels for which they were employed.

These impressed names are often most difficult to read because the metal was removed from the mould before it had cooled sufficiently to have accepted a lasting impression.

The impressed comb flutes will readily be identified by a glance at Plate 2A. Moulded comb flutes are relatively shorter on tall decanters and higher on short vessels. When decanter bases are not made from moulds, comb flutes are sometimes cut upon them.

The scarcity of name-impressed pieces testifies to the fact that the impressing practice was not standard factory procedure; but when name-impressing moulds were used, the provenance of the resulting vessel is frequently (but not invariably) established.

Partial moulding of glass as a built-in characteristic occurs also in the square, parallelogram, oval or round bases of vessels, chiefly salts. The

[1] Westropp, p. 181.      [2] ibid.
[3] Gatchell letters, etc., document 32. The name of Joseph Aldritt (with two t's) has been found in an 1823 Dublin Directory; he had premises at 20 Stafford Street, where he worked as lathe, tool and steam engine maker, but whether his shop is the one referred to in 1832 is uncertain.

employment of moulds for these parts is said to be peculiar to Irish glass. The product resulting from the use of this technique has been referred to as pressed (in hand mould) although in this study the more inclusive and shorter term moulded glass has generally been used. Moulded bases may correspond in shape to the bowl of the body (cf. Plate 81C). Such bases are not solid, as might be assumed, but are moulded with a cavity beneath. The shape of the ribbed cavity has led to the descriptive term of 'lemon squeezer' base or foot. Moulded bases may also be observed on the large-scale boat-shaped or round bowls of which the salts mentioned are smaller versions. On the larger vessels the moulded foot may be ornamented on top with radial ridges generally swirled from the point of origin at the base of the stem to the edge of the foot itself (Plate 39A).

### Neckrings

The rings to be found around the necks of decanters, as well as the absence or presence of a pouring lip, are obviously built-in characteristics.

Neckrings make their appearance with the barrel shaped decanter of late eighteenth century origin. They became a conspicuous feature of the tall tapered vessels of the Bristol-trained B. Edwards of Belfast. In the light of their general use on Belfast bottles, it is interesting that their presence on the familiar Bristol-blue labeled decanter is more the exception than the rule.

There seems little basis for the theory that neckrings evolved because of the heaviness of the filled decanter, already heavy in itself. Neckrings are found on marked, light weight, decanters of slightly more than pint capacity, of the *Cork Glass Co.* (1783–1818), decanters which would not be unmanageable even when filled. However, on Waterford and the later typical Age of Exuberance vessels of tremendous weight even unfilled, they provide a welcome, convenient and comfortable grip for safe handling.

The numerous styles of rings include: the round ring (Plate 8A); the double ring both plain and, in Plate 4C, feathered; the triangular ring (Plate 1); the triple ring (Plate 8B); the square ring (Plate 2A); and the faceted or cut ring (Plate 53A). In the case of the 'feathered' ring, the terms 'notched' or 'ticked' are sometimes used. In the case of the 'double ring', the 'double' refers not to there being two rings but to the fact that each of the 'double' rings (which usually come in pairs or threes) is composed of two small rings made from a single ring lightly divided.

Toward the close of our period, built-in neckrings give way to ornamental neck cutting which provides the safety of grip previously mentioned (Plates 52A, 53B). By this time the tapered and barrel shapes of decanters have been superseded by a vertical, straight sided shape (Plate 52B).

### Pouring Lips

Insofar as pouring lips are concerned, their width generally complements the ampleness of the body of the vessel; they add, along with the neckrings, to the horizontality of the decanter's appearance. Variations to this occur, nor are they confined to the impressed pieces of any one or other glass house. To cite an example, *B. Edwards Belfast*, thought to have specialized in tapered decanters, with triangular neckrings (to the exclusion of other types), and without pouring lips, will be found in the pictures of his impressed examples to have used double neckrings lightly notched and wide lips as well.

This example of lack of factory consistency provides an opportunity to comment on the migration of craftsmen. They moved about from glass house to glass house, carrying stylistic influences along with their skills. This led to repetition of styles among factories and to an inevitable uncertainty where attribution is concerned. Migration of artisans was not confined to the glass makers but occurred with the engravers and cutters as well.

### (b) The Applied Characteristics

Applied characteristics include the work on a vessel by the glass cutter and/or the engraver, and may include the stopper if it is obviously cut to conform with a decanter.

Since cutting and engraving are performed *on the surface* of the vessel, subsequent to its manufacture, they are less reliable means of identification of origin than are impressed bases, profile, lips and neckrings.

For example, when a number of decanters impressed by a given factory are assembled for study, highly individual engraving and cutting motifs become evident and the temptation arises to couple a motif with an impressed factory name and to accept that motif itself as a hallmark or signature. But the presence today of blanks, with impressed names but no engraving or cutting, emphasizes the fact that it was not standard procedure always to decorate at the time of manufacture.

In proof of this there are several advertisements in the *Cork Evening*

*Post*, 1793, and the *Hibernian Journal*, 1777, wherein a Cork dealer ' "supplies Cork and Waterford glass, does the cutting himself, and also employs a cutter from England" ', and one James Armstrong, presumably the Armstrong of Ormond Quay, states ' "he cuts his own glass" '. Definitely, 'Irish glass was cut in other towns than those in which it was made'.[1]

Another example, showing that we may not rely on engraving as a proof of date, concerns the pair of decanters on Plate 48, which have Waterford characteristics. They are engraved with the Waterford name and the date 1782. The Waterford glass house, however, did not open until 1783.[2]

Taking Irish cutting and engraving separately and in that order:

*Cutting*

We have seen how the repertoire of glass cutting of German émigrés, subsequent to the accession to the throne of the first George (1714), met with English approval, was learned by English craftsmen, was enlarged by the addition of cutting variations, and then was suddenly retarded by the imposition of the 1745 Excise Tax on weight. As style changes had demanded ever more elaboration in cutting, a vessel heavier both in section and in scale had been required to sustain the elaboration.

With the emigration of the English craftsmen after Free Trade in 1780 to Ireland, where no weight restriction influenced the further evolution of cutting, history repeated itself and the demand for style changes again dictated heavier vessels and ever more elaborate cutting. The 'Age of Exuberance' was on, and exuberance was not to cease till the 'prickly monstrosities' of the Great Exhibition of 1851 proved that cutting technique could go no further; by then the vessel was deeply cut all over, and the pendulum had reached the limit of its swing.[3]

As we now have in mind the evolution of glass cutting, it is interesting to revert to the advertisement in 1841 by Edward Ronayne's heirs cited in the comments on the Terrace Glass Works. In that advertisement is the first reference encountered in this study to the introduction of steam power to an Irish glass house; its first known introduction into Ireland, however, was in 1818 when the Ronaynes founded their Terrace Works.

[1] Westropp, p. 199.
[2] *Antiques*, June, 1956, p. 522. fig. 2, article: 'Waterford Glass' by R. J. Charleston.
[3] The expression 'prickly monstrosity' was originated by the late Bernard Rackham, distinguished author and one time Keeper of the Department of Ceramics at the Victoria and Albert Museum.

Prior to the introduction of steam, the cutter's wheel was turned by hand by a youth or boy. It was surely a dull, tiresome job and it takes little imagination to assume that as interest or energy flagged so did uniformity in the speed and the revolutions of the wheel against which the cutter was practising his craft.

With the introduction of steam that was changed, and the cutter obtained a uniformity of speed to his cutting wheel previously denied him. Also, *he* now controlled that speed.

Was the introduction of steam power responsible for the decline in cut glass as an art form? The question can be argued both ways: with hand power a truly handcraft product resulted, having the imperfections thereof, or – if you will – an uneven and primitive charm. Whether to be desired or deplored, irregularities resulted from 'a failure in co-ordination between the man who worked the wheel and the man who cut the glass'.[1]

The introduction of the steady steam-driven wheel gave the cutter more confidence in his equipment and in his own skill. As this confidence increased, so did the cutter's virtuosity. The decline in taste in cut glass cannot be attributed to the inanimate machine but to the cutter's (or his public's) insistence upon an ever increasing display of the cutter's mastery of the machine and the scope which the machine provided.

It is interesting to note, in connexion with this steam power discussion, that a 'swag motif rendered by semi-circular cuts'[2] which is found especially in Waterford glass of the John Hill–Jonathan Gatchell period (1783–1799), and which would thus precede the introduction of steam power to Ireland, is 'technically very difficult to execute'.[3] In a word, the most exacting cutting was accomplished under what today would be considered the more primitive conditions.

*Engraving*

It has been stated that with the engraving wheel, the English artisan never achieved the same degree of proficiency as he achieved with the cutter's wheel. Similarly, across the Irish Sea, engraving was always secondary to cutting both in quantity and quality. The words 'clumsily engraved' have been applied to the work of the *Waterloo Co. Cork*, and the work on marked pieces of other houses is equally inexpert and repetitious. Such skill in engraving as may be observed on Irish glass

[1] Thorpe, p. 46.
[2] *Antiques*, June, 1956, p. 525, article: 'Waterford Glass' by R. J. Charleston.
[3] ibid.

was exercised in all probability by itinerant Germans or others attracted from European countries. The renown of Irish glass was established by the work above the wheel, not below it.[1]

## Stoppers

Decanter stoppers are an unreliable applied characteristic for identification purposes. It has been remarked of them that they are more vulnerable to breakage than the bottles for which they were made. The chances of their having been exchanged, or of their not being original, are infinite.

During the period of Irish glass under discussion, stoppers were of two general types, the lozenge (Plate 2A) and the mushroom (Plate 13B). The use of one or another type depended, first, upon the shape of the bottle, and second, on the bottle's cut or engraved decoration. The lozenge is most harmonious with taller, lighter bottles, the ones generally engraved, while the mushroom shape complements the broader based, more bulbous vessels which have a greater degree of horizontality in design.

The lozenge stopper is especially subject to variation in design, some variations being: elongated (Plate 10B); plain (Plate 2A); cut (Plate 7A); pear shaped; cut or moulded to suggest the name target stopper often applied to it (Plate 6A); or pressed with a light grid pattern with horizontal ridges on one side, vertical ridges on the other (Plate 5B); or moulded with radiating flutes (Plate 6C).

Mushroom stoppers are most generally found with moulded radial ridges and grooves on the top of the cap, but are occasionally found moulded or with cutting to conform to the bottle (Plate 12). Mushroom shaped stoppers having a noticeable knop below the mushroom cap and above the shank which fits into the vessel, are particularly harmonious with the heavy Waterford type decanters. The stopper with the knopped shank may be a Waterford Glass House characteristic but it is not confirmed as one to the exclusion of the stopper with plain shank. The detail is illustrated in Plate 13B.

It is impossible to close the discussion about stoppers without a further quotation from that busy letter-writer Elizabeth Walpole. This time she writes from Acragar in Co. Queen's (currently Co. Leix), where she may

---

[1] The reference here is a technical one: normally the glass cutter works 'overhand', pressing the vessel before him on to the revolving wheel (there were also 'underhand' cutters). On the other hand, the more delicate operation of the engraver 'is performed on the underside of the wheel, and the operator in pressing his glass against it has no view of the surface on which he is working'. Thorpe, p. 47.

have resided, since the name so often occurs in her correspondence. Her letter is dated '7th of 4th mo 1834' and reads in part: 'Herewith I enclose thee Sarah Wilson's acct . . .; she has deducted 10d. for a stopper which was charged in mistake in Waterford as the stopper really belonged to her originally. She sent it to Waterford to have a decanter made to it . . .'.[1]

[1] Gatchell letters, etc., document 15.

# 6

# Survey of Marked Vessels

### General

Study of the illustrations begins with marked vessels. These examples with moulded bases, nearly fifty in number and representing five types of moulded glass, are not only indisputably Irish but reliably attributable to specific glass houses.

Only 'typical' examples and significant variations of them are shown; no attempt has been made to illustrate every marked example which has come to hand. Selection between duplicate examples, or examples so close as to be almost duplicates, has been made on the basis of the best photograph for reproduction.

The glass houses whose names most frequently appear on marked vessels are as follows and their work will be considered in the order given:

> **B. Edwards Belfast**
> **Cork Glass Co.**
> **Penrose Waterford**
> **Waterloo Co. Cork**

Six other names are found on marked vessels, in addition to those of the four major glass houses. They are:

> **Francis Collins Dublin**
> **Armstrong Ormond Quay**
> **C.M. & CO.** (for Charles Mulvaney)
> **J. D. A.** (Probably for John Dedereck Ayckbowm)
> **J. D. Ayckbown Dublin**
> **Mary Carter & Son 80 Grafton St Dublin**

The examples bearing these names will be considered at the end of this chapter.[1]

---

[1] The reader is referred to Chapter 8 for explanations about nomenclature of vessels and their presumed use, etc., and to Appendix A for definitions of terms peculiar to glass cutting.

## (a) B. Edwards Belfast

Benjamin Edwards and his son worked from 1776 until 1827, a period of fifty-one years. During this long period of time, it is reasonable to suppose the same moulds would have been used because the son bore his father's name and would be unlikely to cast out usable moulds on his father's death. Yet this survey has produced in point of numbers less than ten examples of Edwards, or marked vessels. All of them are decanters.

In addition to this scarcity of Edwards examples, there is another curious detail pertaining to Edwards. In 1781 in the *Belfast News-Letter* he advertised that he had brought a glass cutter from England, yet among our marked pieces there are no cut examples whatsoever.

In the same advertisement Edwards referred to 'enamelled, cut and plain wine glasses'. Perhaps it was some of Edwards' 'plain' glasses which were among the utilitarian wares later exported to America from Belfast and Dublin?

Since Edwards is known to have come to Ireland from Bristol, it is customary to see in his work in Ireland an influence from his Bristol training. In Plates 1 and 2A it is possible to observe the tall, tapering form associated with the blue labelled decanters attributed to Bristol. However, these Edwards examples in the Bristol style are but two out of eight. In Plates 2B, 3A, 3B, we note increasing divergence from the supposed Bristol–Belfast norm; elongation recedes in favour of a squatter, more round-bodied vessel; and, on balance, the tall, taper shape is in the minority. A chronological order for these Edwards styles cannot be established.

It is interesting to observe that the bases of the decanters in Plates 3A and 3B have the same diameter as the base of the tall vessel in Plate 1, but they are notably shorter bottles.

In Plate 4A the decanter pictured is inconsistent with any of the others so far as its shape is concerned, and with its unique long neck it may be considered an oddity.

It has been stated that the lip of the Belfast bottle 'is very narrow and scarcely projects at all; it differs in this from Cork and Waterford'.[1] We find on examination of our Edwards examples that this concept is not borne out. On the tall vessels (Plates 1 and 2A) the pouring lip is minimized, as aesthetically it should be, but as the bottle becomes more rounded in the body, the pouring lip increases in diameter. By the time we reach examples in Plates 4A, 4B, 4C, the lip is every bit as wide as in the *Cork Glass Co.* pieces we shall presently study.

[1] Thorpe, p. 282.

## B. Edwards Belfast

The most arresting overall difference between Bristol and *B. Edwards Belfast* bottles is that the neckring does not appear in the former, whereas every one of the Belfast bottles carries two rings.

But here again we agree only in part with the accepted notion that Edwards decanters 'usually' have two plain triangular neckrings. Half of our examples do have this feature (Plates 1, 3A, 3B, 4B; the latter is triangular although in the photograph it does not appear so). The neckrings on the other half of our illustrated bottles, however, are of three different styles: the square neckring (Plate 2A); the round neckring (Plate 2B); the double neckring lightly feathered (Plate 4C).

It is possible that the square ring is a previously unrecognized characteristic of *B. Edwards Belfast*; another Edwards impressed square ringed decanter is known to the writer, so the one shown in Plate 2A is not unique.

The statement that the taller decanter usually carries shorter comb flutes is clearly illustrated in Plates 1 and 2A; as the bottle diminishes in height, the comb flutes correspondingly grow higher, as in Plates 4A and 4C.

The most appropriate stopper among the Edwards vessels is that used on the bottle of Plate 2A. The stopper shown in Plate 4A appears too small for that bottle, and perhaps provides an example of the practice of exchange or substitution of stoppers which makes them unreliable guides for identification purposes.

In Plate 4C is illustrated the grid type stopper; on one side the ridges are vertical, on the other they are horizontal. This ornamentation is of course pressed, not cut. Used with these engraved vessels, such stoppers are attractive; it cannot be said whether they are or are not original to their bottles.

Each of the three engraved examples of *B. Edwards Belfast* possesses special interest because for the first time in this study Masonic symbols, a flowered decanter (see below) and symbols of the Union of 1800, are encountered.

In Plate 4A is a decanter ornamented with Free Mason symbols including a square and compass, sun in splendour, moon and seven stars, Jacob's ladder, trowel, crossed quills, plumb rule, crossed spades and the initials J G. The figures 822, referring to the lodge number, are seen through the bottle.

Since this vessel is impressed *B. Edwards Belfast*, no further proof of its being Irish is necessary, but it may be said that the former Free Mason Lodge 822 is now Lodge 46 of Comber, Co. Down.[1]

[1] Lepper and Crosslé: *History of the Grand Lodge of Free and Accepted Masons*

In Irish newspaper advertisements in the late eighteenth and early nineteenth centuries, 'flowered glasses' and 'flowered decanters' were named. In Plate 4B there is a typical flowered decanter. The drawing is freely rendered round the body of the vessel, between the lower neckring and high comb flutes, and the foliage shown appears selected at random and is non-representational, which is not the case in the following instance. In Plate 4C is shown a pair of decanters engraved with the rose, the thistle and the shamrock, symbols which obviously would not have been united in engraving prior to the Union of 1800. The bottles themselves may be of an earlier date. They are light in weight and thin in section.

### (b) Cork Glass Co.

When the writer at one time boasted to a London dealer that he had acquired a pair of marked *Cork Glass Co.* decanters, the comment came back: 'Well, now you can start finding the hard ones.' What the dealer was implying as to the availability of Cork Glass examples has been borne out by the results of the present survey. Whereas there were less than ten Belfast marked vessels in the group of fifty vessels under study, of *Cork Glass Co.* there are thirteen. In addition, so many duplicate examples are available that has not been worthwhile to keep track of them.

There are three distinct types of profiles to the Cork decanters: there is the rounded, full body, as shown in the blank (Plate 5A); there is the more squat type illustrated in Plate 6A; and there is the mallet type as pictured in Plate 8B. The tall, tapered vessel (Plate 7B) is a curiosity because it does not conform to any of the three basic shapes.

Reasonably constant among *Cork Glass Co.* decanters are both a fairly wide lip and triple neckrings lightly notched (Plates 5A, 5B, 6A, 6C, 7A, 8C). But there are variations: the Cork cut example (Plate 7C) has square neckrings and a modest pouring lip; there are three triple neckrings and a modest pouring lip on the mallet example (Plate 8B); and the cut example with engraved initial (Plate 8A) has three round rings and also a modest lip.

---

*of Ireland,* Vol. I, 1925. I am indebted to Mr. Wilfred A. Seaby, Director of the Ulster Museum, Belfast, for this interesting topical reference.

In connexion with this Free Mason decanter, it may interest Free Mason members who are not already familiar with it that there is an extensive collection of glass, much of it engraved with symbols of the Order, in the museum of Freemasons' Hall, Great Queen Street, London. The museum is not open to the public.

## Cork Glass Co.

The bottles which have rather shortened bodies (Plate 6A, 6C) have also the shorter comb flutes observed on shorter bottles from Belfast.

With the *Cork Glass Co.* we encounter our first jug (Plate 6B), a utilitarian vessel with a sturdy loop handle. The long leaf frond, engraved below the rim, makes its first appearance here; we will encounter this device repeatedly, as well as the jug form.

The most consistent detail found on engraved Cork examples is the vesica motif which shows in Plates 5B, 6A, 6B. The vesica is the *Cork Glass Co.* 'signature'.

At their point of joining, the engraved vesica motifs are usually combined with an eight-pointed star (Plates 5B, 6B).

A variation from the standard shown in Plate 5B occurs on one of a pair of impressed *Cork Glass Co.* decanters in New York's Metropolitan Museum of Art (MMA, AC. #24.132.12 a–b). They are not shown here but are generally similar to the decanters in Plate 5B. Although the crosshatched vesica is present in the New York bottles, it is interrupted on one side by a monogram E D enclosed in a leafy wreath open at the top.

The engraving of the rather squat decanter in Plate 6C provides a welcome variation to the recurring vesica theme. Here we have alternating eight-pointed stars and elongated sunbursts between two rows of tiny crosshatchings, forming three bands around the lower shoulder of the bottle, pleasingly emphasizing its shortened body. For the first time in this study an engraved husk pattern is introduced. It is rather freely rendered, circling the upper body.

In the quality of this *Cork Glass Co.* engraving there is considerable variation. The engraved work shown in Plate 6C appears carefully executed; the same cannot be said of the author's pair of decanters (Plate 5B), and even more clumsy is the crosshatching work displayed within the vesica of the jug illustrated in Plate 6B.

In Plates 5B, 6A is seen for the first time a small engraved decoration so slight as almost to elude observation or deserve comment. It consists simply of lightly touched-in engraved dashes, in two bands with varying space between, around the upper shoulder of the body of the vessels, relieving an otherwise unadorned area. These dashes accomplish the same purpose as the more emphatic, though loosely rendered, husk circlet on the decanter of Plate 6C.

Coming now to the cut, in contrast to the engraved, examples of *Cork Glass Co.* impressed pieces, we find they present great variety and are of the most commanding interest.

The decanter in Plate 7A has graceful and well-executed leaf festoons;

they occur below bands of hollow facets, a cutting device which will be seen frequently henceforth. Most often, the bands of facets are not separated but joined together top and bottom (Plate 54A*a*). They occur also in two bands about the upper body of the decanter in Plate 7B. That bottle is unique because the vesica motif, so identified with *Cork Glass Co.*, is enlarged and *cut* upon its surface, not engraved as previously shown. Within the vesica are handsome stars and at the vesica joinings cut splits are observed for the first time as a cutting device.

Similar splits, together with cut stars and a graceful cut swag below two bands of hollow facets, occur again in the decanter in Plate 7C. This decanter will have heightened interest when compared with the *Francis Collins Dublin* example in Plate 20A.

Particular interest attaches to the decanter shown in Plate 8C. The wide circlet of fine diamonds around the shoulder is lovely in itself and especially attractive used in conjunction with the graceful ribbons linking hexagonal medallions. The ribbons are filled with fine vertical cut flutes and the medallions with fine diamonds. The writer has seen, in an old photograph, a similar ribbon-medallion treatment, above which was a cut circlet of husks, but the latter were not so complimentary to the ribbon-medallion treatment as the wide fine diamond band shown in Plate 8C. The fluted target stopper shown with this beautiful decanter is very probably not original.

On the mallet-shaped decanter in Plate 8B are flat, vertical flutes, tapered in width, cut between the lowest neckring and the top of the shoulder. The flute cutting has been relieved by bands, a wide one and a narrow one, of prismatic cutting, encircling the shoulder. Prismatic cutting on a much more elaborate scale will enter into later observations.

The impressed *Cork Glass Co.* examples are concluded with two most extraordinary pieces; both are important but for different reasons.

All three parts of the butter cooler with cover and stand shown in Plate 9B are of the finest metal cut in great perfection with matching bands of medium diamonds. The cover exhibits a button finial on a short plain stem rising from a stepped circular plane. The lower third of the butter cooler itself is cut with flat flutes of uniform width. It is of the first importance that this splendid example is impressed, for while we have had a plethora of decanters and vesica ornamentation from *Cork Glass Co.*, we have not previously encountered a *Cork Glass Co.* object of this type, nor has Cork previously displayed this diamond type of cutting.

Contrasting with the elegance and perfection of the butter cooler, so richly and skilfully cut, is the more humble shallow dish of Plate 9A. This moulded dish is certainly a great rarity and may very well be unique. On the original, the impressed name *Cork Glass Co.* is so extremely clear that some of the letters may even come up in the photographic reproduction.[1]

### (c) Penrose Waterford

It is a curious and ironical fact that the most celebrated name in the annals of Irish glass manufacture is represented in this survey, without resorting to duplication, by the fewest number of marked examples. There are only seven pieces to be shown, six decanters and one finger bowl.

It is probable that all these examples date from the Penrose period of ownership of the Waterford Glass House, that is, from 1783 to 1799. The impressed name on the seven pieces is *Penrose Waterford*. Jonathan Gatchell bought out the interest in the glass house of the surviving Penrose brother in 1799. It hardly seems likely that, having obtained a partnership in the factory after years of apprenticeship to the Penroses, he would have continued to use their moulds.

The seven vessels shown, therefore, may with reasonable assurance be dated prior to 1800. In view of the scarcity of marked Waterford pieces, it is indeed fortunate that in six of the seven exhibits (that is, in all the decanters), a uniform shape is maintained, while the four vessels which are cut have also a highly distinct character.

Uniform among the decanters are the following features: an exceptionally wide pouring lip; a generous swelling body above high comb flutes (less noticeable in Plate 10B); and, in general, massiveness and weight indicating a liberal use of metal.

Of the six decanters, all have three neckrings, and five of the six are of the triple-ring variety. The sixth example has three double neckrings lightly notched, a characteristic it shares with a *Penrose Waterford* impressed bottle at the British Museum (BM 1938 5–2–1, not illustrated here).

Only one of the six *Penrose Waterford* decanters is engraved (Plate 10B). The subject matter is the same as in the *B. Edwards Belfast* of Plate 4C, the rose, thistle and shamrock of the Union of 1800. It is possible that this vessel was made as a blank during the Penrose period

---

[1] Shown with the marked CORK GLASS CO. decanters are four types of stoppers, whether original to their bottles or not. They may be described as (1) the moulded grid (seen above in Plates 4A, 4C, Plate 5B); (2) the plain target stopper with centre depression, Plate 6A; the target stopper with moulded ridges, Plate 6C; the target stopper very prettily cut with centre star and edged with oval cut disks, Plate 7A.

and engraved subsequently to the Union. The engraving is carefully done, the treatment of the rose in particular being far more expertly handled than in the Edwards example, where the petals of the flowers are scarcely delineated.

The cutting of the vessels in Plates 11, 13A, 12, 13B is far more significant than the engraving on the one engraved example. The pillar and arch motifs of the first two, and the pendant semicircle motif of Plate 12, are established as Waterford characteristics because of their consistent presence on these marked vessels. It is to be noted also that the pillar, arch and semicircle are all filled with fine diamonds, and that in the first two examples the height of the pillar varies; it may be either square or rectangular, and the arch too is subject to variation. Two of the four cut decanters have a band of hollow facets encircling the upper shoulder, while the other two have double bands of prismatic cutting.

In connexion with the cutting on the first three decanters, where it involves a curved incision, not a straight one, we may recall that a 'swag motif rendered by semi-circular cuts' has already been referred to (Chapter 5, b) as 'technically very difficult to execute'.

Special interest attaches to the decanter, one of a pair, shown in Plate 13B, because of the feature of the single row of cut strawberry diamonds which encircles the shoulder. From early photographs, this device is known to have occurred on another decanter, also marked *Penrose Waterford*. That decanter had a circlet of cut husks around the upper shoulder, in place of the prismatic cutting in Plate 13B, so there is no chance of that vessel's being the same as the one pictured.

Thanks to these several instances of the single band of cut strawberry diamonds on marked Waterford bottles, the motif is established as a Waterford Glass House characteristic of the Penrose–Gatchell period.[1]

In Plate 14A occurs the first instance of a finger bowl. A similar one to this, also with *Penrose Waterford* mark, is to be seen in the Ashmolean Museum, Oxford (AM, Gift, 1939, Mr. William King). Also known from photographs is another *Penrose Waterford* marked example, also with two notches, which is of dark blue glass.

It is a minor but interesting point that the height of the comb flutes in the finger bowl of Plate 14A is identical to the height of the flutes

---

[1] Stoppers shown with the PENROSE WATERFORD decanters are (1) mushroom type with radial cutting on top combined with concave centre, Plate 10A; (2) elongated target stopper, with a centre depressed area and highly milled edges, perhaps not original to the bottle, Plate 10B; (3) mushroom stoppers, respectively moulded and cut, but each with the preferred knop between the mushroom and the shank, Plates 11, 13B; (4) a stopper cut with fine diamonds suggesting purposeful conformity with the decanter, Plate 12.

made by the mould of the Ashmolean example (45 mm.). The height of the vessels themselves and the diameter of their tops, being affected by hand manipulation, vary slightly.

### (d) Waterloo Co. Cork

The second of the three Cork glass houses and the one whose vessels are found with the impressed name shown above, opened in 1815, three years before the final closing of the *Cork Glass Co. Waterloo Co. Cork* was, therefore, in operation when the *Cork Glass Co.* men were left unemployed, and it is reasonable to assume that some were taken on by the newer Waterloo company.

In fact, by the year 1815 all the important glass houses of Ireland listed in Chapter 4 were in operation except for the last of the Cork houses, Terrace Glass Works.

These facts of chronology become significant when we examine the *Waterloo Co. Cork* impressed examples, because they have very marked resemblances to the impressed examples of earlier glass houses, and especially to examples of their neighbours *Cork Glass Co.* and *Penrose Waterford*.

It is indeed at this juncture that we become most aware of an inter-changeability of characteristics of design among the several Irish glass houses. It is hard to believe that the labour which made the Waterloo pieces did not also make the *Cork Glass Co.* and *Penrose Waterford* ones; although made with Waterloo moulds, the decanters have been created with a strong Penrose similarity where weight, lip, neckrings, body profile, are concerned, and the jugs have been created with an equally close resemblance to Cork's.

But, curiously, regardless of weight, which generally pleads for decoration by cutting, we find Waterloo vessels ornamented chiefly by engraving. And Waterloo engraving has a unique character. Of the ten *Waterloo Co. Cork* vessels yielded by the survey, one is a blank, two are cut, and seven are engraved. Of the seven, six are engraved in the highly individual Waterloo style.

The basic Waterloo decanter shape is shown to advantage in Plate 14B, one of a pair. Here are the wide lip, three triple neckrings and generous swelling body, already observed in *Penrose Waterford* pieces (Plates 10A, 10B, 11, etc.).

But in the bottles in Plates 15A, 15B, 15C, the Waterloo engraved characteristic makes its apperance and is seen in minor variations. It consists of the bowknot and flower motif, the former generally with a loose end of a ribbon depending from it and the latter generally cross-hatched within, after the fashion of *Cork Glass Co.*'s vesica.

The several motifs are joined by a frond motif, more often lightly implied than honestly stated. In the decanter in Plate 15C, however, a different hand has been at work: the frond is better realized, and the earlier dependent ribbon below the knot has become three tassels. The two bottles illustrated in Plates 15A and 15B carry the small engraved dash device in two bands around the upper shoulder, noted in *Cork Glass Co.*'s Plates 5B and 6A, but in the Waterloo decanter of Plate 15C these dashes have been replaced by light hollow facets, further emphasizing that decanter's differences from the preceding ones.

In Plate 15B we have, indeed, a crosshatching very carelessly executed and suggestive of the inferior workmanship observed in this detail in *Cork Glass Co.*'s jug (Plate 6B). Despite this minor difference in the engraving in Plates 15A, 15B, 15C, it is reasonably apparent that they were decorated by the same hand, or to a style which was imposed upon the engravers by the glass house.

Before leaving Waterloo's engraved decanters, however, attention must be centered on the Waterloo decanter (Plate 16A) and the *Cork Glass Co.* example (Plate 6C). Except for the initials I H B with their enclosing fronds, which occur on the former, the engraving treatment is identical. The base of the Waterloo bottle (Plate 16A) is shown in a photograph in Plate 16B; one sees how the comb flutes of the mould, extending down the sides of the bottle are carried along underneath. This particular decanter is of quart capacity and the outer diameter of the circle enclosing the letters is $1\frac{3}{4}$in.).

The Waterloo house, it appears, found jugs to be popular among its offerings, and included in its impressed group are two examples of jugs (Plates 17A, 17B). Both of these exhibit typical Waterloo engraving with minor variations.

Another Waterloo jug, studied in an early photograph, was very close to the *Cork Glass Co.* example in Plate 6B. Frond, star, cross-hatched vesica – all were virtually identical. One was led to believe that despite the difference in name impressed at the time of manufacture, the same hands must have carried out the engraved decoration on both pieces.

Apropos of the shape of these jugs, the form is an interpretation of an English jug form[1] datable to 1760–1770. Since *Cork Glass Co.* and *Waterloo Co. Cork* came into being some decades later than that approximate date, this may be an instance of a time-lag in style between

[1] Thorpe, Plate CLVII, 1.

English and Irish work, or it may be an example of a long retention of a form because of its basic practicality.

The shape of the Waterloo decanters in Plates 18A and 18B which are cut, not engraved, is essentially that of *Penrose Waterford.*

However, the decoration of the first decanter consists of a combination of motifs from both Cork and Waterford: below the familiar and normal hollow facets in two rings are the cut vesica and splits of *Cork Glass Co.*'s decanter in Plate 7B, with the star motif therein replaced by a Waterford type strawberry diamond.

The Waterloo decanter of Plate 18B is so close a replica of the Penrose bottle shown in Plate 11 as almost to make one believe an error in labelling has occurred.

In summary, all major Irish glass houses were in operation when Waterloo opened, except Terrace. Also Waterloo outlasted Williams and perhaps Mulvaney of Dublin, Edwards of Belfast, the Penrose phase of Waterford, and the Cork Glass Co. Waterloo was in a good position to 'borrow' from the others, and indications are that that is just what it did.

### (e) Miscellaneous Names on Marked Vessels

The remaining examples of marked vessels represent the small group of persons or companies whose precise role in the Irish glass manufacturing-distributing system is unresolved.

With the exception of Charles Mulvaney, represented by an impressed *C. M. & CO.* piece, who is believed to have manufactured briefly but known to have had a later connexion with the manufacturers, Jeudwin, Lunn & Co., Dublin, all members of this group are presumed to have been primarily purveyors of glass. References in contemporary records are generally to their warehouses, suggesting a distributing function. We may recall the young John Wright's correspondence with his brother Jonathan, wherein he mentions '. . . the retail Ware room on the Quay (which is my department) . . . now becomes a separate establishment quite distinct from the Glass House. . .'.[1] But that was in Waterford: which, among the glass houses working in Dublin during our period (Williams, Mulvaney and/or Jeudwin Lunn, Chebsey), actually manufactured the glass for these persons and firms is an unanswered question. It is also entirely possible that these presumed distributors placed their orders with glass houses out of Dublin, where terms and quality were more to their liking.

[1] Gatchell letters, etc., document 18(a).

*Francis Collins Dublin* is the most amply represented in this group because there are four types of vessel bearing his name.

The first is a finger bowl (Plate 20B). This example does not have the notched rim which is exhibited in the *Penrose Waterford* finger bowl (Plate 14A), but it is otherwise very similar. Nicely engraved on the Collins piece is a crowned harp below a curved ribbon, the latter carrying the words 'Loyal Dublin Infantry', thus emphasizing Collins' affinity with the capital city. The metal of this finger bowl is exceptionally fine.

*Francis Collins Dublin* is represented also by a two-lipped finger bowl with long pointed leaves pendent from a horizontal line just below the rim (Plate 19A). The use of this neo-classical motif, so satisfactory for the embellishment of the high, plain wall of the finger bowl, has been observed on contemporary silver.[1]

The butter cooler, one of a pair, shown in Plate 19B, is another Francis Collins piece which has particular interest. The lower part of the base is fluted by mould as in the finger bowls mentioned above, but the upper part of the base has been widened to accept the lid which thus rests *inside* the bottom section. This detail of design will be often encountered. The flattened knob finial will also be seen repeatedly.

The interest which attaches to the *Francis Collins Dublin* impressed decanter in Plate 20A is due both to its shape and its cutting. Glancing back to the *Penrose Waterford* impressed decanters (Plates 11, 13A), it will be noted that the Collins decanter in Plate 20A has three typical Waterford features; the wide lip, the three triple neckrings, and the generous swelling body, all built-in details. Yet if we also glance back to our *Cork Glass Co.* decanter in Plate 7C, it will be seen that the Collins decanter in Plate 20A has the identical cutting of the Cork one.

The evidence suggests that the Francis Collins bottle may have been made from his moulds at Waterford, and later ornamented by an accomplished glass cutter working in all probability in Dublin.

The Francis Collins pieces are uniformly of good quality, whether made in Waterford or in Dublin.

*Armstrong Ormond Quay* is represented by a single example, the decanter in Plate 22A. It is of interest because of its Bristol type tapered neck, its absence of pouring lip, and because of the two *triangular* neckrings which occurred in half of the *B. Edwards Belfast* examples. It is to be observed, though perhaps it is not significant, that the only previous instances noted of elongated vertical flute cutting, below the lower neckring and above the shoulder line, was in the decanter from

[1] MacLeod, *Journal*, p. 142.

*Cork Glass Co.*, Plate 8B. The Armstrong example is a little fancier than the Cork one because the neckrings while triangular (not clearly to be seen in the photograph) are facetted, the first instance of this treatment, and the long flute cutting is terminated with horizontal cuts.

The evidence of the lack of lip, of two neckrings and the lengthened profile, suggests that an Armstrong mould was used by a Belfast factory, and that the cutting was done by an itinerant or Dublin glass cutter.

*C. M. & CO.*, for Charles Mulvaney & Co., Dublin, is represented among the impressed examples by the single dish in Plate 21B*b*. Its base and sides are moulded, its edges cut in a generous scallop design. It is a substantial but utilitarian piece of glass, a meagre reminder of what was 'confessedly the most extensive manufacturer in Ireland'.[1]

*J. D. A.*, for John Dedereck Ayckbowm, is best considered simultaneously with Mulvaney because the example of *J. D. A.*'s work which we have is a dish almost identical to Mulvaney's. It is one of a pair, and is shown in Plate 21B*a*. The picture was taken to show both the moulded rayed base and the side decoration suggestive of heavy slanted gadroons. There is a slight difference in size between the *C. M. & Co.* and *J. D. A.* vessels.

A finger bowl impressed *J. D. Ayckbowm Dublin* (Plate 21A) is the only vessel to bear his name and surname in full, in contrast to the pair of dishes bearing the initials *J. D. A.*

*Mary Carter & Son 80 Grafton St Dublin* is represented in the Plates by a two-lipped finger bowl (Plate 22B). Except in the detail of a more meagre lip, it is very similar to the first doubly lipped finger bowl shown, which bore the name of *Penrose Waterford* (Plate 14A).[2]

---

[1] Westropp, p. 55.

[2] According to an article (MacLeod, *Journal*, pp. 141 *et seqq.*), describing the marked finger bowls believed to be of Dublin manufacture in the collection of the National Museum of Ireland, the vessels may be listed for reference as follows:

| Marked Name | Description |
| --- | --- |
| **Francis Collins Dublin** | 2 plain bowls: 1 engraved (note A below) |
| | 1 plain |
| | 2 two-lipped bowls: |
| | 1 engraved (note B below) |
| | 1 plain |
| **Mary Carter & Son 80 Grafton St Dublin** | 1 two-lipped bowl: plain (note C below) |
| **J. D. Ayckbown Dublin** | 1 two-lipped bowl: plain (note D below) |
| **Armstrong Ormond Quay** | 1 two-lipped bowl: plain (note E below) |
| Note A: Ill. our Plate 19A | C: Ill. our Plate 22B |
| B: Ill. our Plate 20B | D: Ill. our Plate 21A |
| E: Handsome dark blue in colour. | |

# 7

# Examples with Coins and
# Irish Silver Mounts

In addition to mould-marked vessels, indubitably Irish, there are two small groups whose Irishness may be considered equally assured. One group consists of vessels with coins whimsically imprisoned within their stems, the other of glass vessels with identifying Irish silver hallmarks or engraving.

The coin in the stemmed and covered bowl (Plate 24) reads: 'Bank Token-Tenpence. Irish 1805' and on the reverse it carries the head of the King and the words 'Georgius III Dei Gratia'. The lid has a swirled rib-moulding below a knop finial; within the cover, under the finial, there is a pontil mark. The cover fits inside the bowl, as seen in the Francis Collins butter cooler in Plate 19B.

The bowl, in turn, is characterized by a threaded decoration around the rim, while around its lower part an outer layer or gather of glass has been superimposed upon the inner vessel. The result achieved by this treatment is not unlike that of the slanted gadroons on the Ayckbowm–Mulvaney moulded dishes (Plate 21B*a*, *b*).

The coin in the mug (Plate 23) reads: (obv.) 'Georgius III Dei Gratia Rex', and (rev.) 'Bank Token 10 Pence Irish 1813'. In this example a heavily threaded decoration surrounds the rim, while the lower part of the bowl is even more heavily adorned with gadrooning. This vessel is remarkable for its size. Both it and the preceding example have plain round bases.

Both pieces are obviously of the nineteenth century, yet with their threaded rims, plain circular bases, and the gadroon decoration of the mug, they are closely related to English examples dating from between 1700 and 1750.[1]

There appears to be no explanation of why these early, out-of-date styles were still being followed during years which could not have been previous to 1805 and 1810 respectively. The thought comes to mind that with his economic freedom to use metal generously, the Irish craftsman

[1] cf. Thorpe, Plates LXXVI, bottom, 1, and CIX, top, 2, and same, bottom, 1.

B. Standing bowl of blue glass with 1844 coin in clear stem. Height $5\frac{3}{4}$ in. Ulster Museum, Belfast. (See page 81)

chose from personal preference to follow these forms which require a notable quantity of metal.

The sugar bowl of Bristol blue (Colour Plate B) contains within its clear glass stem an 1844 half-farthing coin. The bowl came to its present Museum collection from a Belfast source. The tradition passed along with it is that it was made by one 'James Ronnax in the Glass House, Graham's Place, Ballymacarrett, Belfast, for his (Ronnax's) great great grandmother'.[1] Unfortunately the name of James Ronnax does not appear in the relevant literature.

Because of the blue colour, the city of Bristol comes at once to mind as the place of origin of the bowl. But blue glass was neither a secret nor a monopoly of the English city. It will be recalled that Benjamin Edwards, Sr., removed from Bristol to Belfast, that he 'imported' a glass cutter, and it may be supposed that other Bristol craftsmen, whether migrants or permanent settlers, were attracted to his first glass house or Belfast factories of later date. Reason suggests that the manufacture of the bowl in Belfast is more likely than its manufacture in Bristol and subsequent importation to Belfast.

The coin in the bowl's stem would have been in general circulation in Ireland in 1844. It is a British coin and not specifically an Irish one because the Union of Ireland with England was effected in 1800 and the two currencies were amalgamated in 1821.

We show the bowl, probably a family commemorative piece, with a measure of confidence in the Ronnax tradition as it is supported by these other considerations.[2]

There are three examples in the group of glass-and-silver pieces of indubitably Irish origin.

The urn shaped vase with silver top (Plate 25) stands 7¾ in. high. The domed cover with its anthemion pierced design is by William Bond of Dublin, 1797. The wide tapered vertical flutes, above and below the delicate circlet of short upright flute cutting, are reminiscent of Irish work observed in impressed vessels. The small flutes recall the fluted swags seen in an impressed pair of *Cork Glass Co.* decanters (Plate 8c), and will be frequently encountered in the following chapter. The

[1] Museum case label.

[2] This is perhaps an example of the telescoping of generations in family tradition, mentioned in our Introduction. Unless his competance in glass making was achieved by James Ronnax at a remarkably early age, it would seen unlikely that he would have made a piece of glass for his great-grandmother, a relative it is given to few individuals ever to know. The gift of innocent hyperbole belongs as well to the Irish as to antique vendors.

muffineer has a facetted knop above the scalloped foot which is cut with flat flutes to conform to those on the body.

The harmony which exists between the silver cover and glass vessel makes it unthinkable that the former was not designed especially for the latter.

The covered jar shown in Plate 26, in an inverted pear shape with circular foot, is cut all over with a complicated pattern of flat hollow diamonds of varying sizes and shapes. The silver top, with its berry finial, scrolled bracket handles and inverted acanthus border, bears the engraved crest (the moor's head) of the Drogheda family, whose family name was Moore. Although the prominence of the family in Irish history is recorded as early as the mid-1700's, Charles Moore was created Marquess of Drogheda in the peerage of Ireland in 1781, just when the Age of Exuberance of Irish glass was beginning.

As in the case of the muffineer previously noted, it seems outside the realms of chance that this Drogheda vessel with its strong Irish attributes is other than an Irish piece ornamented by an Irish silversmith who beautifully complemented the vessel with his highly wrought decorative top. It was at one time the largest of a set of three identical jars.[1]

The silver frame of the splendid centrepiece shown both assembled and in detail (Plates 27A, 27B) bears the Dublin hallmark for 1787 and the initials CH.[2] Decorating the pierced shield supports are the arms of the Onslow family. There are at present fourteen pieces of glass in this centrepiece (a fifteenth may have filled the top centre oval silver bowl); ten of the fourteen have silver fittings. Three variations of the urn-shaped vase, noted in the preceding muffineer, are here exhibited in sifters, and another variation on the theme is seen in the set of four cruets, one of which is shown in a close-up (Plate 27Ae). These vessels are identical in their types of cutting and vary only in the scale of the relief diamonds and the length of the vertical tapered flutes noted also in the muffineer (Plate 25).

This centrepiece is very clearly a luxury glass production, wherein the weight of the metal used (and also cut away) was of no financial importance. From that point of view the glass parts might possibly have

[1] The smaller pair was destroyed in World War II. It is recorded the pieces were 6¾ in. in height.

[2] There were two silversmiths named Christopher Haines working in Dublin 1784–1794. They were father and son, and registered, respectively, in the years mentioned in accordance with the Statute 23 and 24 George III. C. 23 (Ireland 1783). Considering the Dublin hallmark of 1787, the centrepiece may reasonably be attributed to Haines, Senior. (Jackson, Sir Charles James, *English Goldsmiths and their Marks*, Macmillan, 1921.)

originated in England about the year 1787. On the other hand, glass used in conjunction with metal and with cutting such as displayed in these cruets, is characteristic of Irish work at this time. It has been said that 'silver and plated stands were imported (to Ireland), and, as at Waterford, were fitted with bottles at the glass works'.[1] In his *A History of Old Sheffield Plate*, Frederick Bradbury comments on 'the enormous quantity of plated wares sent into Dublin', many to be equipped no doubt with Irish glass fittings.

Thanks to its hallmark, we know this centrepiece was not imported but made in Dublin. While it is perhaps claiming too much to declare Dublin the place of origin for the glass as well, Dublin is a possible place and Ireland is certainly a most probable one.[2]

[1] Westropp, p. 105.

[2] It may be of interest that an almost identical silver mounting as shown on the cruet in Plate 27A*e* is illustrated in F. Buckley, Plate XLII, captioned 'Later Cruet Bottles, 1780–1800.' He shows no cruets or sifters with the exuberance of the examples in Plate 27B, but since small single vessels of this type are in reasonable supply among antique dealers, Buckley's comments (p. 85) may be of value to the inquiring collector.

# 8

# Examples of Irish Glass

The arrangement which follows of the various types of vessels is frankly arbitrary; articles of larger size and general household use precede articles related to the dining table, drinking, the flavouring of food, etc. Toward the close of the chapter we treat briefly miniatures and miscellaneous pieces which lend colour, variety and human interest. A chronological order within each group of articles has been attempted but has been impossible always to achieve.

## (a) General

*Covered Urns*

The covered *urns* discussed in this section are of a generous size and are not to be confused with smaller covered vessels here termed *jars* and included later under articles for dining table use.

Except perhaps where ewers are concerned, the classicalism, or classic influence, in eighteenth-century Irish glass, is nowhere more clearly discerned than in the covered urn. In the eight examples shown, classicalism runs the gamut from a first chaste spired vessel (Plate 28A) to a last exuberant article bearing little resemblance to its predecessor (Plate 33).

The beauty of the urn in Plate 28A is achieved by an understatement of decorative cutting. In this respect the urn is less obviously Irish than any of its kind. In addition, the sprig and oval engraved device is reminiscent of English work. However, the device is not exclusive to England; it may be seen in Plate 56, on a ewer with marked Irish characteristics, and again in Plate 69A, on a covered jar with handles which has a Belfast provenance. In addition, the details of the facetted finial and the tapered flat cut flutes on both parts of the urn, are found repeatedly on Irish work. The reason this urn does not have the exuberance expected of Irish glass, to be seen in all the following examples, is no doubt because it is the earliest in the series, about 1785–1790.

The second urn (Plate 28B) is one of a pair. It exhibits much the same profile, except for the foot and stem, as the urn in Plate 28A, yet it has important differences of a very Irish nature. Now there are a deeply prismatic, facet cut finial, the familiar tapered flat flutes, and an important band of flutes in vertical edging around the rim of the bowl. Coupled with these cut devices are leaf ornaments in rows on top and body.

In the pair of urns in Plate 29 the severely classic urn has acquired marked elaboration in its cutting. While vertical edging flutes, and flat tapered flutes (gently interrupted by prismatic rings), and a row of husks are now present, for the first time single and double bands of large shallow diamonds appear. All of these motifs are rendered very flat, imparting a limpid quality. These jars are pellucid but they are very heavy in actual weight. They are star-cut beneath, testifying to a date of about 1800. or later. They have a slightly blue cast of colour.

On the massive urn of Plate 30A, which is notable for its height of $11\frac{1}{4}$ in.), large shallow diamonds are used to the exclusion of any other cover or body decoration, barring the stepped circular planes below the finial and above the stem. Notable in this piece are the short, thick, flat fluted stem and the heavily stepped base from which it rises. As in the case of the last pair of urns, this piece is somewhat blue in colour.

In the urns of Plate 32, broad fields of large shallow diamonds are relieved by vertical flute edging and wide flat flutes both above and below. The flattened finial complements the somewhat depressed cover outline and an annular knop between the vase proper and its stem will be noted.

In the remaining examples of the covered urn the apogee of Age of Exuberance vessels in this group is reached. All are richly cut all over with a repertoire of devices many of which have not previously appeared.

In the vessel of Plate 30B, return is made to the formal and familiar covered urn shape, highly domed with a sharp pointed finial, but the cut diamonds are now medium and sharp. Deep and wide panels are present, filled with the sharp diamonds, while above and below the panels are cut swags – uniformly looped, deeply incised, forming the panel partitions.[1]

The set of three covered urns (Plate 31) presents very curious features. The distinctive button finials are on very high shanks which are so plain one almost wonders if they were not unintentionally left unfinished: the vessels are otherwise most elaborate. Both tops and bodies at their rims are vertically fluted so that at the joining there is no projection or overhang: this has been reserved for a place high

[1] This covered urn was dated by Thorpe as '*c.* 1800'. *Antiques*, November 1930, p. 411. article: 'The Development of Cutting in England and Ireland, Part II'. The urn was illustrated. In view of the two late examples shown in Plates 31 and 33, the present writer believes 'about 1820' is a more likely date to assign to it.

up on the cover, where it has no practical function. Most interesting of all, however, are the swags filled alternately with medium, plain, sharp diamonds and fine slanting flutes. Several rows of cut swags fall below the filled ones. These vessels might be dated about 1820, a date in line with that of the Waterford Service with which they have a strong affinity (see Plates 89A, 90B, and Chapter 10).

There is a family resemblance, in addition to the exuberance of their cutting, which exists between the preceding three urns and the final example of the covered urn (Plate 33). Obviously it lies in the fluted vertical edging of both covers and bases. This wide decorative detail separates the upright and inverted Gothic arches. The massive stepped circular plane of the top of the cover is repeated under the body before the flat fluted stem proceeds into the stepped and square base. These areas where body meets finial and, below, where body meets stem, are very suggestive of the massive neckrings on Waterford impressed decanters. To be noted also are the fluted fans with which the cutter filled what he must have regarded as unbearably empty spaces.

We see in this piece a first example of the 'international style'; the strawberry diamond, while closely associated with the period 1820–1840, was not exclusive to any one factory, city or country. However, the urn's finial, colour and quality suggest an Irish origin, possibly Cork or Dublin. The urn may be compared with pieces from the Wellington Service (Plates 91–92C).


*Candlesticks*

In the candlesticks shown in Plate 34B there is a characteristically Irish lavish use of metal in the tall shafts. An extravagant amount of material had to be cut away to achieve the deep prismatic cut effect. In this particular the shafts are in contrast to those of many English candlesticks of the middle and latter part of the century; while frequently tall, they were thin; knops in their stems were modified and appeared as cusps, etc. The flattened foot of the candlesticks in Plate 34B, with its elongated printies, departs also from English examples, which were domed with an instep frequently cut with a geometric design.

The printie, a usually circular concave motif, is said to have derived its name from the practice of grinding away from the base of a vessel the pontil mark which was left when the puntee iron was detached. It is more obviously displayed in the jug in Plate 57.

The classic influence on Irish glass design, seen in covered urns, is apparent again in the vase in the candlestick in Plate 36. This candlestick, one of a pair, is remarkable no less for the completeness of its numerous parts than for the distinction of the parts themselves. A pronounced Irish characteristic is the deeply cut trefoil rim[1] of the sleeve which holds the candle and which slips into the standing socket. This sleeve is, in effect, the candle's *bobêche*; a second ornamental *bobêche* fits over the socket, rests upon the wide flange (see Plate 35A for a similar example), and has six points, each with two pendant cut lustres.

Akin to the previous example is the classic vase candlestick in Plate 35A. Here, medium, plain, sharp diamonds encircle the body in a band and divide vertical flat flutes. This use of a diamond band constantly recurs in Irish work. The moulded base contains the ribbed cavity previously referred to as 'lemon squeezer'.

Short candlesticks of the type shown in Plate 35B are rare. Features of this pair are the hollow ball knops of the stems, cut with medium bands of large shallow diamonds, and the generous cylindrical sockets with their cut flat flutes. The flat circular foot is cut beneath with rays, the rays extending from a smooth polished centre as in the case of the urns in Plate 32; this treatment suggests a date of about 1820 or a little later. Except that they are so short, these candlesticks might possibly have been equipped with removable parts which rested on the socket flange and carried pendant lustres. Single and double candleholders, somewhat taller than these and heavily encircled with prisms or lustres, come into use about the date of these, and have circular bases not dissimilar to the bases seen in Plate 35B. Such candleholders, however, do not appear to have been made in Ireland; the stubby ones with their cut ball knops in Plate 35B may well be their Irish precursor.

The significant Irish detail about the candlesticks in Plate 34C is the cut vertical edging of the drip pans (cf. Plate 32), of which special mention was made in the Introduction. The metal of these pieces is of the greatest brilliance and suggests that they were subjected to fire polishing, a practice of reheating the finished article to remove marks of the marver or glassmakers' tools. It results in providing exceptional sheen. Notwithstanding this, the infrequency with which one notes fire polishing suggests its use was a corrective one and not one used purposefully to achieve a heightened effect.[2]

---

[1] The trefoil rim is also known as the Van Dyke rim, and is supposed to have taken that name from the lace in portraits by Sir Anthony Van Dyck.

[2] A distinction is here drawn between the reheating of a gather while an article is being made, to maintain the plasticity of the metal, and the reheating of the finished glass before placing it in the annealing oven. Pellatt makes reference to both processes; McKearin is the more explicit about fire polishing.

All glass holders were not of luxury or cut glass type. There were also moulded candlesticks, made with features resembling cut glass articles and frequently moulded sticks were partially cut to modify the moulded look.

A typical pair of moulded candlesticks is shown in Plate 34A. They have ground circular depressions beneath the square bases; 'lemon squeezer' cavities are more usual. They have non-removable candle sockets with plain rims; occasionally removable sockets were used, and these in turn are sometimes seen with a modified trefoil cutting. The melon form introduced into the stems of the pair illustrated is found sometimes elongated, sometimes tapered toward the bottom, sometimes slightly twisted. The grooves are generally more pronounced than suggested.

Inspection of the examples in Plate 34A will show that on removal from the mould the lower platform bases have been cut square and polished, in contrast to the upper platforms which have the soft appearance of melting ice cream.[1]

## *Vases*

Turning next to a group of five vases, Belfast origin is claimed for one, Cork origin for a second, Waterford origin for a third and fourth. For the fifth no city of origin can be affirmed with confidence, but the vessel is indisputably Irish; it might be of Dublin or late Cork origin. The Belfast and Cork examples have every appearance of being commemorative drinking vessels. The other three are generally called celery vases although their shape would permit any number of other contents.

The provenance of the high, stemmed example in Plate 37A and 37B is obviously Belfast because that name is engraved upon it. The date of the engraving is likewise given, 1802. On one side are engraved the initials T B and on the other side a spinning wheel. Both motifs are contained between crossed branches of olive and bay, familiar emblems of peace, of conquerors and heroic fame. The identity of T B is not known, but linen industry annals might reveal him as one prominently identified with the triumph of the Union of 1800.

The mechanical crosshatched bands, boxed stars, etc., with which the

---

[1] The moulded candlesticks seen in Plate 34A were probably made by a primitive method, evolved by local craftsmen, using sectional moulds for the several parts of the stick. The candlesticks have no mould marks indicating seams nor have these been removed.

It is very probable that in the different glass houses variations of combined mould and hand manufacture were employed as experience and knack dictated.

out-turned rim of this vessel are engraved, seem inconsistent with the grace of the major decoration and prompt the thought they may have been engraved by another hand than the one which executed the commemorative work.

A vessel of gargantuan size is the commemorative piece shown in Plate 38A. It is both cut and engraved. The cutting occurs, it will be noticed, where the metal is thickest, while the engraving occurs high up on the vessel where the bowl terminates in a rim which is comfortably thin for drinking. The name John Billington and the date 1813 are engraved on the bowl. Billington is said to have been an actor, to have played in Cork in 1813; and this vessel is supposed to have been given him on that occasion.[1]

Very characteristic of Irish work is the turned-over rim; the first vessel seen with this feature in this study is the heavy vase shown in Plate 38D. The rim of this piece suggests *Cork Glass Co.* (cf. Plate 9B); the foot and lower body of it also suggest Cork, as seen in the mixing glass in Plate 75D. The straight sided shape indicates a late date, perhaps 1825–1830, because the straight side tended to replace the curved side about that time. This is especially to be noted on decanters seen in the Samuel Miller drawings.

With the two remaining vessels of this group firm grounds exist for asserting Waterford origin.

In the vase of Plate 38C there is a circlet of the deep swags filled with fine diamonds which were seen on the impressed *Penrose Waterford* decanter in Plate 12; in this connexion we are reminded that 'a continuous semicircular pattern pendant from a straight horizontal line, the semicircles filled with fine diamond cutting . . .' is observed as '. . . commonly employed in the Waterford glass-house. . .'.[2]

As if this were not enough, it can be said that the metal of this piece is brilliantly clear, that the workmanship of the scalloped rim, slanting blazes, short flat flutes and drapery swags is impeccable.

Although the pendant semicircles of this example in Plate 38C appear in the Samuel Miller drawings used from 1820 onward, I am inclined to

---

[1] This is a case where historical confirmation does not support legend. The Billington-as-actor story was promulgated in the Catalogue of the Walter Harding Collection. However, *The Journal of the Cork Historical and Archaeological Society* yields no reference to Billington. In *Musical Memoirs 1784–1830*, by W. T. Parke, reference is made to a 'Mrs. Elizabeth Billington, the singer . . . married early to James Billington . . . an excellent double bass player at Drury Lane.' The *Dictionary of National Biography* refers also to 'her (Mrs. Billington's) brother-in-law Thomas . . . d. 1832' and 'a third brother Horace was an actor.' No references have yet come to light as to John Billington, actor.

[2] Westropp, p. 196.

give this piece an earlier date because of its limpid beauty and under-statement of cut decoration. This belongs, I believe, to the *Penrose Waterford* period of impressed, swag-cut decanters, – the best Hill–Gatchell period (1783–1799), and not to the exuberant period illustrated in the next example.

For the exact prototype of the vase in Plate 38B we have only to turn once more to the Samuel Miller patterns. Here are the identical knopped stem and the bowl with slanted sides. The sides are cut with prismatic rings interrupted by vertical prismatic cuts, making small squares filled with cross cut diamonds. (The latter are clearly visible in Plate 79D.) Obviously this vessel may be dated from 1820 and it is probably considerably later. This is a rare example of almost positive identification through the Waterford pattern sheets.

Prismatic cutting has hitherto been encountered only incidentally; in the vase in Plate 38B it plays a major role in the cut decoration. Since it will occur with increasing frequency, it is suitable to pause here to discuss it as a cutting device.

There is evidence that some prismatic cutting was employed in England for luxury goods after, as well as before, the Excise of 1745. Because it required such thickness of metal, however, its real development occurred in Ireland, not in England.

There is no evidence that prismatic cutting was a technique exclusive to one or another Irish glass house. However, in addition to requiring thickness of metal, prismatic cutting also required the finest *quality* metal if it was to be used to best advantage. The *Penrose Waterford* glass house led the other glass houses in quality of metal during the years John Hill and Jonathan Gatchell were the technical men in charge. The case for Waterford as being a prime user of the prismatic cut is further supported by reference to prismatic rings *in the instructions* accompanying the Samuel Miller pattern drawings.

It may thus be deduced that the period of prismatic cutting ranged from the late eighteenth century through the 1820's and 1830's.

On the vase in Plate 38B prismatic cutting is used vertically and horizontally. When bowls are considered in the next section, it will be seen used diagonally, when double and even triple cuts across one another. Prismatic cutting is most frequently employed upon vessels in the round: the decanter in Plate 50A is an example, as well as the covered jar in Plate 68C. It lends itself well to the underside of flaring lips of ewers (Plate 54C) but may also be seen on the flat underside of a plate (Plate 77B). Finally, it appears as the sole decorative cutting device for a complete dinner service (Plates 87A–88B). It is in such instances, when the metal is of prime quality and the work carefully executed upon objects thick in section, that prismatic cutting imparts the appealing look of silver.

*Bowls*

Between the years 1783 and the close of our period, about 1835, the glass bowl was made in Ireland in a wide variety of both shapes and cutting styles. Barring decanters, there is no other group so large. Here an arbitrary division has been made separating large bowls from smaller ones, and in this section the larger bowls will be reviewed.

It is notable that all of the bowls shown are decorated with cutting; none is engraved. Engraved bowls which can confidently be considered Irish have not come to hand.[1] It is true that earlier bowls, the late eighteenth century ones, lent themselves to engraved decoration because they were comparatively thin in section, but cutting of a very flat, shallow character took precedence over engraving.

The classical influence upon Irish glass is apparent again in the oval bowls illustrated in our Frontispiece and in Plates 39A and 39B. These are variously termed salad bowls, fruit bowls, lemon bowls, boat shaped bowls. Their moulded bases (e.g., oval, as shown in Plate 39A, and square) and the classical vase stem (as shown in the Frontispiece) have already been noted as characteristic of Irish glass. Bowls such as these do not appear to be of Waterford origin but may be assigned to Dublin or Cork, most probably the latter.

At a glance these bowls have strong resemblances, but the following differences will be noted. The example in Plate 39A is utilitarian, having a firmly attached, heavy, baluster stem. This is not the case with the Frontispiece bowl or the one in Plate 39B. With these the bowls are not attached, but are balanced upon their bases. Again, whereas the Frontispiece bowl has its classic urn stand, the stand in the example of Plate 39B is tubular, oval above to accommodate the oval bottom of the bowl, rounding out towards its middle but spreading towards an oval shape again at the base. All rims are different, the scalloped rim in a generous version (Plate 39A), the very lightly pointed scalloped rim (Plate 39B) and the characteristically Irish trefoil rim in a splendid interpretation (Frontispiece), all being represented.

[1] There is a type of stemmed, knopped and covered waisted bowl on a round domed foot, which is commonly engraved: Buckley, F., *A History of Old English Glass*, Plate XLIII, 1, shows one; another has been exhibited at the Metropolitan Museum, New York (Ac. No. 24.132.14 a,b). Both examples are engraved. Although these bowls are said to be of Irish origin, I do not know on what grounds. They are, in any event, prior to our period.

The bowl cutting of Plate 39B is modest; splits, pointed up and down, separate the units of a single band of large hollow facets. Three double bands of the same encircle the tubular stand. Somewhat more elaborate is the cutting shown on Plate 39A. Here will be seen the same splits but now they are separated by diamonds alternately filled with cut stars and flat, medium, plain diamonds.

All of the motifs on these three examples (Frontispiece, Plates 39A, 39B) are rendered very flat. They thus contribute to the engaging limpid quality which the bowls have in common. Speaking generally, this flat cutting, while not exclusive to Irish work, is one of the more obvious hallmarks of Irish glass of the late eighteenth century, just as diamonds in their numerous forms and depth of cutting (sharpness) are characteristic of glass of the nineteenth century.

A type of bowl which is peculiar to Ireland is the circular bowl with tripod legs (Plate 40A). Such bowls are both novel and extremely rare. They are sometimes seen with turned-over rims with alternate prism cutting, and the treatment of the foot also varies.[1] The deeply cut trefoil rim, observed several times heretofore, was popular from the 1780's until early in the nineteenth century. The example shown in Plate 40A is the most unusual bowl of this type which the writer has seen, its outstanding feature being the bent leg which flattens out into a foot terminating with toes. All the cutting motifs on the side of the bowl are characteristically Irish.

Another exceptionally bold, trefoil-rimmed bowl on an unmarked silver rack is shown in Plate 40B. On this bowl the reader will discern a variety of cutting devices in addition to the notable rim.[2]

[1] A plain pad foot is illustrated in Westrop, Plate XXXIX, top, 2, facing p. 188, and another example with legs terminating without feet as on a simple stool is shown in Hughes, on. 278, facing p. 344, described p. 349. Both examples have turned-over rims.

[2] The rack seen in Plate 40B is especially fine with its spiralled frame supports and twisted ribbon swag motif in two scales. Less pretentious rims for Irish glass were made in quantity of Sheffield Plate, in which connexion the following quotation is of interest: 'So far none of the old Sheffield plated catalogues, issued for general trade purposes, have disclosed any illustrations of the so-called Irish styles of shaped or pierced dish rings (or dish rims). This fact would naturally lead to the conclusion that they were made exclusively for the Irish market.' Bradbury, Frederick, *A History of Old Sheffield Plate*, Macmillan, London, 1912, p. 276.

Such Sheffield rims were sometimes made reversible; oval on top, circular on the bottom, to fit oval or round glass bowls. The date for these rims Bradbury gives as 1795 and 1800, which is about right for trefoil rim bowls. Often bowls have outlived their racks, presenting by themselves a curious appearance. They should be recognized as incomplete articles, however attractive the bowls themselves may be.

Two bowls, from an English point of view 'needlessly extravagant' with the metal used in their domed bases (Plates 41A, 41C), now follow. On the first, the tubular stem is of note. On the second, the turned-over rim already noted as an Irish characteristic (on the late celery vase in Plate 38D) is seen again.

Another example of the turned-over rim bowls is seen in Plate 41B. There is no area of this bowl which is not cut. About the edge are sharp medium diamonds, and these are repeated on the lower body; also, flat broad flutes appear; both these characteristics recall the *Cork Glass Co.* impressed butter cooler in Plate 9B. The stepped square base of this turned-over rim bowl is star cut beneath, suggesting at once the late date assigned to it.

Another bowl with turned-over rim is seen in Plate 41D. This bowl is important because of its moulded sides with rim turned over by hand manipulation. Here again is a vessel which combines in its manufacture the several techniques mentioned in a footnote on page 88. Used on this bowl are two decorative devices borrowed from cut glass: vertical prismatic cutting separating fields of diamonds. These devices, in minor variations of size and sometimes horizontal as well as vertical, constitute the limited Irish repertoire where moulded vessels are concerned. They occur again in decanters and in celery vases with turned-over rims.[1] In bowls such as the one illustrated, there is a thickness of section which results in a nearly smooth interior surface while on the outer surface the moulded pattern is raised to the touch. But it is not, of course, as sharp as it would be if it had been cut.

In the short waisted bowl on circular base, shown in Plate 41E, there is a foretaste of splendid things to come, for the fine diamond-filled swags relate to the Corporation of Waterford dinner Service in which such swags play so important a role (Plates 89A–90B). The double row of large hollow facets show to good effect in this photograph and the band round the body of the vessel, with its cut stars, should not be overlooked. This bowl, though footed, may be thought a precursor of the hanging lamp bowl, an example of which is shown in Plate 86C.

With the bowl next illustrated (Plate 42B) there occurs another of those extraordinarily happy pairings of a glass vessel and its equivalent in the Samuel Miller pattern sheets. Bowls of this type are often called 'kettle drum' bowls.

---

[1] In American Blown Three Mold glass, especially in decanters, one finds a wider repertoire of moulded panel patterns. The American designs have been exhaustively classified and shown in diagrams in their numerous variations by George S. and Helen McKearin: see Bibliography.

The next two somewhat smaller bowls (Colour Plate C and Plate 42A) are of approximately the same date and dimensions. They have been selected because they illustrate the late Irish characteristic of double and even triple prismatic cutting, crossing to form strawberry-filled diamonds. The waisted bowl in the Colour Plate has a turned-over rim, while the rim of the other example has fan scallops lightly serrated. Prismatic cutting, together with fans and fine diamonds, decorates the underside of the circular base of the example in Colour Plate C, while the same area of the piece in Plate 42A is rayed.

Unusual interest attaches to the yellow bowl of Colour Plate C because of the method by which the colour was achieved and because of the colour itself. The vessel has been 'stained'. Examination of a small chipped area reveals that colourless glass lies below the yellow surface, which is evidently a 'yellow stain', produced by silver-oxide. The scarcity of such 'stained' glass suggests it was very seldom produced in Ireland. What small amount there is of coloured Irish glass resulted from colouring the entire mix of a pot of metal so that vessels made therefrom would be coloured throughout, not upon their surface alone. Receipts for making blue glass and green glass will be found among the formulae given by John Hill to Gatchell (Appendix D, 'Receipts for Making Flint, Enamel, blue and Best Green Glass, etc.'). While blue and green Irish examples are scarce, yellow pieces are more so and the stained yellow example may very well be unique.

The example in Plates 43A and 43B is more remarkable than beautiful but doubly remarkable for being intact although intentionally in two parts. In this piece Irish exuberance is rife, with strawberry diamonds, fine diamonds and a fan-cut rim. And in addition to these essentially Irish cutting devices, the now familiar device of prismatic cutting is used round the neck of the base. The flat dish is equipped with a flat circular boss on its underside; this fits the open top of the lower section The surface of the boss itself is cut all over with fine diamonds. The weight of both pieces, and especially of the dish, is great; without such weight this means of joining the two parts would be precarious indeed. The example illustrated came from Bangor, near Belfast. Another example, also very similar in shape but quite different in cutting, with a reliable Irish provenance, is in the collection of the Marquess of Bute; still another version of this bowl and stand, from the collection of the Duke of Wellington, is shown in Plate 91A. The latter, it will be observed, has a turned-over rim.

*Decanters*

All decanters previously discussed bore the impressed names of factories. We come now to a more eclectic group; the vessels themselves are more varied and, it might be said, more diverting because of the diversity of their shapes, engraving and cutting.

The first example is a carafe with a strong Co. Down provenance, initialed D. G. J. for Down County Jury (Plate 44C). In the same collection with it is another of the same shape but engraved with the circled shamrock device of the Down Hunt. A ewer of unusual shape (Plate 44A) shows this shamrock insignia, while the decanter (Plate 44B) carries a device of an encircled recumbent hare, also associated with the Down Hunt. It will not be overlooked that the decanter has three triangular neckrings.[1]

In the next three examples (Plates 45B, 45C, 45A), all of which may be dated late eighteenth-early nineteenth century, there is uniformity in the treatment of the neckrings; all are of the triangular variety. Otherwise the rings vary from two to three in number, the tapered bottle with minimal pouring lip becomes more generous and a medium lip appears on the final example. The first is the only one which is cut; perhaps it may be attributed to Edwards' imported glass cutter. If he did cut this decanter, he prettily combined long flat tapered flutes with cut swags, and also he *cut* the comb flutes round the base of the vessel. This is the first instance of such cut flutes instead of moulded flutes.[2] The name Irwin on the bottle in Plate 45C is a familiar one in Ulster.

In Plate 45A appears a first example of an engraved crowned harp on which might otherwise be termed a flowered decanter. The style of this engraving is unlike the style of other Irish engraving considered 'typical'.

The tall decanter in Plate 46A is in no respect related to Edwards nor can it be confidently attributed to Belfast. It has, however, a strong topical Ulster connexion, being engraved with the words 'The Bush-mills/Old/Distillery/Co Antrim/Ireland'. The factory trademark is

---

[1] It is a matter of commanding interest that the obvious Ulster provenance of this glass is supported by Down Hunt account book records in which occur entries such as '1785 Edwards & Shaw, Belfast, Decanters and Glasses as per acct. £5.3.2'; '1793 Mr. Edwards bill for Glasses ect. (*sic*) £4.17.4'; and '1795 Cash pd Edward's bill for Glassware £4.9.1½.' See also note 2, page 130, for another reference to the Down Hunt account book records.

[2] One other example with long flat tapered flutes cut upon the elongated neck of a bottle has been noted at the National Museum of Ireland, Ac. No., 83-1907. It presents much the same profile as in Plate 45B, but the comb flutes are moulded and the pretty cut swags are absent.

centred between these words and wreaths of shamrock. The date for this decanter is variously placed between 1820 and 1850; the latter dating is perhaps preferable. Unfortunately Company records yield no historical background.[1]

The vessel illustrated in Plate 46B, engraved 'Success To The/Cork Yeomanry', presents an enigma. It is engraved with an apparently typical *Waterloo Co. Cork* crosshatched flower, yet Waterloo did not come into existence until 1815 and the date of 1796 is ascribed to the decanter.[2]

The next two decanters have special significance (Plates 47A, 47B). The former descended to the late Captain Alfred Graeme MacMullen from the Penrose family. By tradition, this graceful bottle belonged to Elizabeth Penrose, daughter of William Penrose and great-grandmother of Captain MacMullen. It is easy to accept this tradition, for the bottle is engraved with – among ribbons, flowers, etc. – a pen and a rose rebus and three intricately rendered initials the last of which is unquestionably the letter P.[3]

Another Penrose rebus decanter is shown in Plate 47B. On both sides of the bottle are engraved roses and quills.[4]

The richly engraved decanter in Plate 46C very strongly suggests in its profile the slightly less tapered *Cork Glass Co.* vessel shown in Plate 7A. The same high comb flutes are apparent as are also the three lightly

[1] The 'Old Bushmills' company has written in correspondence with the author that 'a number (of such decanters) have turned up . . . the most recent having been found in the California desert'. (Two other examples may be found more readily in the Ulster Museum, Belfast.) The Bushmills writer was of the opinion that the decanter was a 'Christmas package job, probably supplied to special customers' and was 'certainly not shipped as part of a set contained in a wooden case'. However, squares were indeed made in sets of two, four and six bottles and enclosed in partitioned wooden containers.

[2] The date of 1796 is based upon the fact that in December of that year Bantry Bay was the threatened scene of a French invasion. The towns of Cork, Galway and Limerick were united in plans to repel it. The landing never took place owing to unfavourable weather conditions, and the invading fleet returned to Brest, but the expected role of the Cork Yeomanry was manifest and the illustrated decanter was probably a unit presentation piece.

[3] Elizabeth Penrose married, in 1805, Anthony Robinson (b. 1779) of Moate, Co. Westmeath; their daughter, Susannah Penrose Robinson, married Joseph William MacMullen of Cork; their son, Alfred Robinson MacMullen was the father of Captain MacMullen. Several more examples of glass of Penrose origin survive in this family (see Plates 52B, 74A, 82A, 82B).

[4] A decanter which appears to be a mate to the Elizabeth Penrose one so far as profile, flat tapered flute and comb flute cutting are concerned, is in the National Museum of Ireland, Ac. no. 16–1935. It is engraved with the initials F S P, for Francis Penrose, a third brother to George and William. It also has the rebus of the pen and the rose.

C. Waisted bowl of glass stained yellow. Diameter 5⅝ in. *c.* 1820–1830. The Pilkington Glass Museum, St. Helens. (See page 94)

feathered neckrings and the medium pouring lip. On the other hand, the engraved bowknot design seen through the vessel and the swags so reminiscent of those on the decanter of Plate 15C and the fronds of Plate 16A, both of which are impressed vessels, suggest that this may have been a *Cork Glass Co.* bottle decorated by a *Waterloo Co. Cork* engraver.

In the *Liberty* decanter (Plate 47C) there are moulded high comb flutes, generous body profile, double feathered neckrings and small lip, all suggestive of the pair of Edwards impressed vessels in Plate 4C. Since that is all there is to go on, any attempt to assign this piece to a particular factory would be mistaken. But since it is engraved with an American eagle and the words 'American Independence', in addition to the word 'Liberty', its Irishness is scarcely open to doubt and, obviously, it must be dated after 1776. Because it conforms in character with Free Trade glass house vessels, its probable date is post-1783.[1]

The pair of decanters engraved 'Success/To The/Waterford Volunteers/1782' (Plate 48) presents another enigma. Except for a slightly full body, the outline here has the characteristics of a *Penrose Waterford* bottle: very wide lip, three triple neckrings, generous profile, moulded comb flutes of appropriate size. Yet the *Penrose Waterford* glass house, which produced so many bottles akin to this one, was not founded until 1783.[2] The date 1782 is presumably commemorative.

At the end of this group of notable decanters comes the pair of bottles engraved 'The Land We Live In' (Plate 49A). Below the legend, in a circle, are the initials IWE. On the reverse sides of the bottles the Union symbols have been disposed in a novel design rendered very freely. The shamrock occupies the centre space on the body of the vessel, while it is framed left and right by the rose and the thistle. All three symbols are visible at one time, which is seldom the case with round vessels. A trace of gilding remains on the bottles.

There are two notable features of the decanter shown in Plate 49B, C. The first, because it is the most obvious, is its size. It is characterized by a straight sided, softly shouldered profile; it would seem to have a long neck but for the two strong round rings which break its line, and it has a

---

[1] W. Buckley illustrates this decanter, Plate 102-B, in a section entitled 'Irish Glass'; on his p. 93 he describes it 'Made in Ireland circa 1780', which date appears today a little too early.

[2] This discrepancy in time was mentioned in *Antiques*, June, 1956, in an article 'Waterford Glass' by Robert J. Charleston, wherein one of the vessels was illustrated. Buckley, W., illustrates one of the two, Plate 102-B, in the 'Irish Glass' section of his work, and on p. 93 describes it as one of 'a pair of Waterford blown glass decanters with stoppers . . . Made in Ireland. 1782.'

suitably scaled pouring lip. Its globular stopper, to judge by the harmony of its design with that of the bottle, must certainly be original.

The second feature of this vessel is the topicality of its engraving. While on one side it bears the framed words of the loyal toast, 'The Glorious' And Immortal Memory Of King William III/Our True Deliverer,[1] and an equestrian figure; on the other it reads 'Loyal/ Dungannon/Orange Society', lettering attractively embraced by curved branches of olive and oak. The Dungannon Orange Society was formed in 1796 in the linen-making town of that name in Co. Tyrone; it is about fifty miles west of Belfast. The bottle thus has an Ulster provenance. It will be recalled that the Edwards, father and son, carried on their Belfast glass house through the first quarter of the nineteenth century, and also that Edwards, Senior, had started his Irish career at Drumrea, a colliery town near Dungannon.

All the remaining decanters illustrated are cut, not engraved. They constitute a splendid resumé of late cut work. They emphasize the use of motifs already familiar but combine them in new ways, and – in several cases – introduce cutting motifs not hitherto used.

As shown in the decanter in Plate 50A, with its spectacular conforming spire stopper, the prismatic cut is combined with a wide band of vertical pillar flutes. These are cylindrical columns in half section with the curved side facing out. They require the same lavish use of metal as prismatic cutting, and for that reason their development took place in Ireland subsequent to 1780. 'Lustre cutting' is considered a debased term for pillar-flutes, which are shown extensively in the Samuel Miller drawings. The combination of prismatic and pillar-flute cutting in this decanter, of high quality metal and workmanship, goes far toward suggesting a late Waterford origin for it. Its date is perhaps as late as 1820–1830, taking into account the Miller patterns.

In the decanter shown in Plate 51A there is a variation on the pillar

[1] Very little of the glass commonly called Williamite falls within the period of this study. But because this decanter and certain glasses to be noted later are Williamite pieces it is suitable to append a note explaining the mystique of William III. At the time of his death in 1702 he enjoyed the maximum of personal popularity. His personality lived into the eighteenth century, even through the 1780–c. 1835 period of Age of Exuberance glass, in an ever thickening aura. From being the successful leader of a cause, William became the symbol of causes. It was a period when loyalties were expressed graphically and glass was a logical medium on which to inscribe a name, date and motto, or to express an avowal. The magnum decanter in Plates 49B, 49C reflects this characteristic of the times as well as the gargantuan consumption of beers, wines and spirits; the engraved figure of William shows how his 'image' had changed through the years from that of a spurred military commander to a laurel crowned figurehead – 'Our True Deliverer'.

and arch motif observed in the marked Penrose Waterford bottles in Plates 11, 13A. The proportions of the motifs are altered, especially the height of the pillar, but the fine diamonds appear and the shape of the bottle, its neckrings and wide lip also conform. It will be noted, however, that in the impressed examples the comb flutes are moulded, whereas in the example of Plate 51A they are cut.

In view of its similarities to marked pieces, one might be inclined to consider this decanter, one of a pair acquired in Dublin, to be of Waterford origin. Remembering, however, the example in Plate 18B which, although it bore similarities to impressed *Penrose Waterford* bottles, was in fact impressed *Waterloo Co. Cork*, one hesitates to assign the present bottle to a particular factory. It might be Waterford or it might be Cork.

Accepting the single band of strawberry diamonds as a hallmark of *Penrose Waterford* design (see Plate 13B and related text), the next two bottles (Plates 50B, 51B) might be assigned to that factory. It would be particularly easy to make such an attribution for the bottle in Plate 50B, for all other features of lip, neckrings, comb flutes and generous, swelling body profile, conform to known standards.

The issue, however, is more clouded in the case of the richly cut bottle in Plate 51B, and one need only turn to the marked decanter from the *Cork Glass Co.* shown in Plate 7B to see why. Now there is a repetition of the cut vesica motif, with star enclosed, imposed on a Waterford style vessel similar to the blank from that factory shown in Plate 10A, and with the added Waterford feature of a band of cut strawberry diamonds. Again, it is impossible to affirm a factory for such a decanter as this. With its dual personality perhaps the best that can be said is that it is doubly Irish.

It is to be noted that all four of the mallet shaped decanters shown in Plates 52B, 52A and 52C are straight sided, have heavy lips, wide flat shoulders; and where neckrings are omitted, they are compensated for by deep prismatic cutting (Plates 52A and 52C). As the necks of the bottles have shortened in these nineteenth-century styles, the neckrings (Plate 52B*a*) are reduced to two in number from the usual Waterford three. The decanter shown in Plate 52B*b* is virtually identical to one in the Samuel Miller pattern sheets (cf: Plates 95, 96); while the one in Plate 52C is an interpretation of the vessel drawn horizontally on the pattern sheet page. Motifs on other decanters in this group may be found variously disposed among the drawings, except for the inverted fans on the decanter in the Plate 52B*a* which, curiously enough in the case of so familiar a device, is omitted from the drawings.

The stoppers in Plates 52A, 52C are particularly interesting for two reasons: first, because they conform to the vessels' body cutting, and second because, with one very indistinct exception, stoppers are completely omitted from the Samuel Miller patterns. The latitude thus given to the glass man suggests he was expected to create conforming stoppers. The stoppers illustrated are happy results of this latitude.

The three decanters on Plate 53A, 53B, 53C obviously belong to the early- to middle-nineteenth-century decades, by which time the emergent international style had made attribution to a specific country extremely difficult. The three decanters, however, illustrate many if not all the cutting motifs in common Irish use in the latter half of the eighteenth and the early nineteenth century. Also, while straight sided decanters predominate on the Miller pattern sheets, there are several examples in which the full bodied vessel profile occurs (Plate 53A). So while these vessels cannot be credited to a particular factory, their root characteristics are Irish, and so we classify them.

These three late bottles exhibit, however, both the 'formal heaviness' characteristic of nineteenth-century British glass, as well as a tendency for cut decoration '. . . more often arranged horizontally than vertically',[1] also described as a Regency characteristic.

*Ewers and Jugs*

Considering what has politely been termed 'the hard-drinking habits tacit in the native (Irish) character',[2] it is logical that ewers and jugs should follow next after decanters. Spirits, wines, including port, burgundy, claret, as well as beer and ale, were consumed in very generous quantities. The export trade in glass to the Continent of Europe (Spain and Portugal in particular) and to Jamaica and the West Indies, no doubt reflects a reciprocal import trade in wines, port and rum. Label decanters suggest the presence of these beverages on dining tables and sideboards. Barley heads, hops, grapes, grape leaves and vines, were – in addition to Williamite, Freemason and Union symbols – common in the repertoire of the glass engraver.

The similar but not paired jugs acquired in Dublin and illustrated in Plate 54A*ab*, appear to be Irish-made, an attribution based upon other

[1] Wakefield, p. 20.

[2] Seaby, p. 1. Drinking habits among all classes of eighteenth-century Dublin are interestingly discussed in Maxwell, Constantia, *Dublin Under the Georges*, Faber and Faber, London, 1936, and are also portrayed in Appendix C, Excerpts from *A Frenchman in England*, 1784, the latter being relevant where Anglo–Irish customs are concerned.

examples found in Ireland of vessels in this shape and supported by typical Irish cutting which they all display. As shown in Plate 54A, a half-dozen motifs can readily be identified. It is all of the flat, limpid style previously associated with the *Cork Glass Co.*

If the vessels are of the *Cork Glass Co.* they must ante-date its closing in 1818. Because of the unclipped, turned-over, lower end of the handles, they might be somewhat earlier than 1818; later handles are generally smoothed off. These handles are very substantial, being well affixed at the top where the greatest strain occurs, and they contribute to a utilitarian character which is less conspicuous in the following vessels.

The two jugs in Plates 54B and 54C, unlike delicately balanced ewers, sit four-square on ample round bases. Any propensity to tip is minimized, but the vulnerability of their pronounced spouts places them quite definitely in a luxury category. Both of these have Irish provenance. The only comparable example the present writer has seen has the heavy pillar flutes associated with the Waterford Glass House.[1] The shape does not appear to have been made in England. Both are, therefore, attributed to the Waterford Glass House. This attribution is based on the known characteristics of that house: the quality of the metal and of the cutting, and the cutting devices themselves (pillar flutes, Plate 54B; prismatic cutting, Plate 54C; fields of medium plain diamonds, both examples; each feature should be taken into consideration with the other two).

Before moving on to the relatively high drama of ewers, we should glance at a vessel (Plate 57), unique because it exhibits printies to excellent advantage. Printies in small oblongs were seen as an incidental motif on a candlestick base, but here on the body of this jug they predominate. Longhand instructions regarding 'sloping rings & printies' occur in the Samuel Miller patterns.

Classicalism or classic influence is discerned as clearly in ewers as in the covered urn. As we approach the Irish interpretation of the classical ewer shape, a further word should be said on this 'classic influence'.

The character of English glass had been profoundly affected by the influence exerted by European immigrant craftsmen at the beginning of the eighteenth century. No further major influence upon English taste and style was manifest until the influence of Greek and Roman architecture, ornament and artifacts pervaded architecture, interior design and the decorative arts. The impact upon glass was less pronounced than upon other decorative arts; it was, precisely speaking, 'an influence' where glass was concerned, not 'an imitation'. Thorpe dates the trend in

[1] Westropp, Plate XIX, bottom, 2, facing p. 92.

England to 1766–1777, a period when the English glass manufacturer was working at a disadvantage. The classical impact upon glass in Ireland came somewhat later and was manifest in the post-Free Trade period.

The vessels in the four plates (Plates 55A, 55B, 56, 58), to which the descriptive term 'claret jug' is generally applied, exhibit profiles of marked 'classical influence' and grace. All are approximately a foot in height; they stand on circular bases considerably smaller in diameter than their bodies, which are generally not very ample; or if ample (as in the ewer in Plate 55B), the cutting is intended by its verticality to give a visual effect of height.

In fields other than glass the delicious, graceful, classic shape was notable in its eighteenth-century imitation for an understatement of applied ornamentation. Similar restraint was not practiced by Irish glass cutters as the Age of Exuberance progressed; this was clearly seen in the case of the covered urn, where the lightness and balance of the early vessel (Plate 28A) was replaced by an excess of ornamentation in the later one (Plate 30B). In this subordination of form to surface decoration, the ewer fared better than the covered urn.

Three of the four ewers carry cut decoration only; in the case of the inverted helmet shaped example in Plate 56, engraver and cutter joined forces; engraved motifs are employed to fill the wide area between upper and lower rows of cut wide, tapered, flat flutes. In the case of the ewer in Plate 58, one of a pair, the body area is generously filled with cut drapery swags, uniform and graduated looped incisions below pendant swags. Both of these ewers may be dated prior to 1800, a dating based in part upon their facet cut handles which are indeed complementary to the ewers they adorn.

Both of the ewers in Plates 55A and 55B have plain handles (except for thumb rests), but both are so distinguished by shape that no further interest is needed: the unadorned high swan neck handles measure up well to their classic origin (cf: the silver handle of the cruet, Plate 27A). Pillar flutes and prismatic cutting upon the neck of the ewer in Plate 55B, and the alternating panels of pillar flutes and medium sharp diamonds, executed both horizontally and vertically, on the example in Plate 55A, testify to a post-1800 date which might extend as late as 1820.

It is a curious and lamentable fact that no ewer is shown on the Samuel Miller pattern sheets. But even without support from that source, on grounds of quality of metal, the types and quality of the cutting, the last (Plate 58) and the first two (Plates 55A, 55B) of these ewers may be attributed to the Waterford factory.

Before turning from ewers, it should be noted that vessels very similar in their classic shape to the preceding are found, on occasion, equipped with stoppers. If the stoppers are missing, evidence of grinding on the inner part of the neck may be seen. In the stoppered vessel the pouring lip is less pronounced and the throat is correspondingly smaller than in the non-stoppered one.

In Plate 55C is seen a pair of stoppered ewers wholly decorated with prismatic cutting and wide areas of sharp medium diamonds. Accompanying them is a matching pair of decanters. All four of the stoppers match, having a swirled cut design composed of grooves and panels, the latter filled with fine diamonds. Such companion pieces as these are unquestionably parts of a service, and – in such impeccable condition – are of great rarity.[1]

Tall stately ewers on small pedestal bases were luxury pieces, whereas six inch jugs with broad flat bases were adapted to more general household use. They had greater utility value than the claret ewers but they were not mean. It may be recalled that in the late eighteenth-early-nineteenth-centuries we are still treating in Ireland of 'that Golden Age of good design, where hardly anything was made without the impress of good taste, allied with superlatively competent craftsmanship . . . and lucid common sense'.[2]

In Plate 59A there is a vessel which strongly suggests the marked *Cork Glass Co.* jug of Plate 6B and its *Waterloo Co. Cork* equivalent shown in Plate 17B. The marked examples, however, were engraved, while the four unmarked jugs (Plates 59A, 59B, 60A, 60B) are cut. The vessel in Plate 60A has a body cut with a variety of motifs associated with *Cork Glass Co.* and they are rendered very flat (see Plates 39A, 39B).

*Salvers*

Salvers are circular rimmed plates on a hollow pedestal base or on a stem with spreading foot, and they descend in direct line from Venetian antecedents. Advertisements in Irish newspapers indicate that they were made in Ireland as early as 1734 and the cutting upon the example shown (Plate 61A) indicates that they were made at least as late as

---

[1] *Antiques*, March, 1950, p. 203, illustrated a matching set of two stoppered ewers and six decanters in three graduated sizes from the collection of Mrs. George A. Garrett of Washington, wife of the one-time United States Minister to the Free State of Ireland. In that pair of ewers, the spouts were pronounced. The set was datable to *c.* 1800–1810.

[2] John Gloag, *Georgian Grace*, p. 3, Macmillan, 1956.

1790–1800. Beyond the latter date the Age of Exuberance begins and the salver does not lend itself to exuberance in cutting.

Salvers were used as trays for wine glasses and glasses of syllabub, custards, jellies (see Plate 75B). They were used singly, but also in matching sets of two and three, arranged in pyramidal form on dining or side tables. Examples exist of salvers with revolving trays on stationary bases, recalling the 'lazy susan'.

## (b) Table Use

*Serving Dishes and Serving Bowls*

Serving dishes, of which three are shown in Plates 61B, 62A and 62B, are of a size to preclude individual use and are characterized by a wide, flat flange. The examples illustrated are just under a foot long and the $2\frac{1}{2}$ in. flange on the dish in Plate 61B may be taken as typical.

The example shown in Plate 61B most obviously illustrates the Irish cutting devices which have been associated with Cork (Frontispiece, Plates 39A, 39B). This dish, and its two companions as well, may be dated to the late eighteenth century; their scalloped edge may be seen as the precurser of the fan-cut scalloped rims which are frequently seen on the exuberant glass of the nineteenth century.

The examples in Plates 62A, 62B, relate to the dish just described because of their size, their flanges and wide, tapered, cut flutes extending on the undersides from the rims toward the centres. Both these examples have an Irish provenance.

The detail of the flutes beneath is interesting because, in the dish in Plate 62B, the appearance of which very strongly suggests its being unfinished, those flutes constitute the only flange cutting other than the scalloping of the rim. While the base of the dish seems to have been completed, the flange does not.

This dish is important because of the light it throws on cutting techniques. The need for the glass man to map out his design is apparent; it will be seen that the geometric outline progresses two scallops at a time except for two single, unbalanced interruptions to the rhythm; these are unnecessary because there are in fact an even number of scallops. Had the pattern been drawn on the dish before cutting was begun, this irregularity would not have occurred. The pattern mapped in advance of cutting, on the covered jar in Plate 69B, is of interest in this connexion.

In two of the three examples of serving dishes (Plates 62A and 62B), there are round spots. Such minute irregularities may be air bubbles or small bits of unfused silicate, and 'are a most helpful guarantee of antiquity'.[1]

Sometimes *stands*, which serve the function of saucers under bowls, are mistaken for serving bowls themselves. This mistake is unlikely to be made in the case of the bowl shown in Plate 63A which is one of a set of seven matching pieces of five different lengths ($5\frac{1}{2}$ in., $6\frac{7}{8}$ in., $8\frac{11}{16}$ in., $11\frac{1}{4}$ in., $12\frac{3}{4}$ in.).

An omission of careful drawing before cutting is evident again on the bowl in Plate 63B, for the star-filled vesica is very much off centre. For this piece it would be impossible to suggest a factory of origin with any assurance; the temptation exists to suggest *Waterloo Co. Cork* because the bowl is so very composite in its motifs; if that factory did make it, the vessel would not date before 1815.

The boat-shaped dish illustrated in Plate 65B was one of a pair, and the idea comes to mind it was part of a made-to-order service. With its prismatic cutting and panels of fine diamonds, it suggests an early-nineteenth-century date. The cutting devices used are known to have been employed in Waterford at that time and the quality of the metal and workmanship are of the first order. Both this dish and another boat-shaped one in the Wellington Service (not illustrated) have been referred to as cucumber dishes.

The octagonal bowl shown in Plates 64A and 64B has no uncut outside surface. Its decoration has been achieved solely by the use of those two recurring cutting devices in the Irish repertoire, prismatic cutting and medium plain diamonds. The thickness of the metal employed is seen in the photograph of the side view. This bowl is more allied to the preceding example than to those which follow; although it is cut all over, the decoration is simple and organized. It comes close to an Age of Exuberance excess, but is – by comparison – modest.

We plunge now into true Age of Exuberance glass. The next three examples (Plates 66A, 66B, 66C) illustrate familiar motifs of cutting carried to a point hitherto unknown, and also show these motifs in a variety of combinations. The cutting is deep, restraint has been abandoned, and the excesses of the international style are apparent.

Of the bowl in Plate 66B, there are three sizes; the largest is $11\frac{1}{2}$ in. long, the next $9\frac{7}{8}$ in.; the smallest $7\frac{7}{8}$ in.; obviously they were part of a service.

In Plate 65A is seen an example of a fan-scalloped edge on a bowl of excellent metal cut meticulously with medium plain, but very sharp, diamonds. The combination of the cutting and the metal of this piece suggest a Waterford Glass House origin for it.

[1] Thorpe, p. 303.

The deep bowl with unusual vertical sides, Plate 65C, appears to have no counterpart and its intended use is unknown. It is of beautiful metal and craftsmanship, the cutting being of the style we have associated with Cork (cf. Plate 39B).

In the bowl of Plate 67A the arch panels filled with medium plain diamonds, which were noted in the late decanter in Plate 53C, occur again. This piece, which is perhaps intended as a sugar bowl, has an Ulster provenance – Newtownards, Co. Down – and it may well be a product of one of the Belfast factories which worked during the first third of the nineteenth century.

In considering the covered serving bowl in Plate 67B one must look backwards to the cutting motifs of the three bowls in Plates 66A, 66B and 66C, and look forward to the covered bowl in the Corporation of Waterford Service (Plate 89A). It is thought this bowl may be part of another service, more of which it is hoped will come to light. Bowl and cover are in the late Irish, international style; it was from such examples as these that reproductions were made, with variations, which gave rise to the title of 'American Waterford' mentioned in our Introduction.

*Covered Jars*

No group of glass vessels embodies more Irish characteristics than the small covered *jars* which are here differentiated from covered *urns*. These characteristics are discernible in both vessel design and cutting; among the former the most obvious are the button finial and the way in which the cover rests within the spread rim of the base.

These jars are variously called preserve jars, honey pots, jam pots, pickle jars, butter coolers. The prevalence of butter coolers, among surviving examples of high quality suitable for dining table use, is explained in the comment 'many English people take it (butter) at dessert', made by la Rochefoucauld (Appendix C). The numbers of small covered jars which one sees today reflect the late-eighteenth to early-nineteenth-century demand for food seasoning with spices which will be noted again when sifters are considered.

The high domed covered butter cooler in Plate 68A, for which a date of 1800 is suggested but which may be a little earlier, recalls at once the impressed *Penrose Waterford* decanter in Plate 13B, because of the strong factory characteristic of the single bands of strawberry diamonds encircling the body and cover.[1] It is interesting to compare this covered

[1] The writer is indebted to Mr. G. H. Tait, Assistant Keeper of the Department of Medieval and Later Antiquities, British Museum, for drawing his attention to a letter by Westropp in which this piece is discussed.

jar with the *Francis Collins Dublin* impressed example in Plate 19B. The comparison again illustrates how the marked pieces may be used to confirm a provenance suggested by design and cutting features. Assuming that the covered jar in Plate 19B was made in the Waterford Glass House, we may reasonably entertain the idea that Waterford was the source of the *Francis Collins Dublin* glass. The high quality of Collins pieces was noted in Chapter 6.

The covered butter cooler in Plate 69C is distinguished by prime quality of metal and workmanship. Especially to be noted as Irish characteristics of design are the wide flat flanges of both stand and cover, the dome of the cover (cf. Plate 19B), and the up-turned rim of the bowl within which the cover rests. The bands of diamonds on the waisted bowl, cover and knop recall the same treatment on the marked *Cork Glass Co.* example in Plate 9B. *Both* the top and under-surface of the cover's extremely thin flange are cut.

The covered jar of Plate 68D is one of a pair acquired in Dublin. Their chief interest lies in the slanting and perpendicular blazes used on both cover and jar. The blazes are not used incidentally but are the most conspicuous part of the decoration. The vertical rows of flute edging, one on each part, repeat a treatment noticed in the large covered urns in Plates 31, 33.

For the jar in Plate 68C there is justification in using the term honey pot. In addition to the beehive shape there is even a notch cut into the cover for the spoon. This pot brings to mind the prismatic decanter in Plate 50A. That decanter was attributed to the Waterford Glass House and dated 1800, possibly later, and the same approximate date would obtain for this very heavy jar, which is also attributed to the Waterford factory.

A covered jar with shields or Gothic arches (Plate 68E) recalls both the Age of Exuberance decanter in Plate 53A and the covered urn with the same motif in Plate 30B. In the present piece, with its decoration so perfectly scaled, arches occur on both the cover and base, as in the urn, but here they are alternately filled with fine and strawberry diamonds. Its decoration, all from the familiar Irish cutting repetoire, is accomplished with great skill and makes this jar, with its splendid clarity of metal, one of the most tasteful examples of the exuberant period.

The covered jar in Plate 68B, which is only 7 in. high, is markedly similar to the covered urn of Plate 28B, which is 11 in. high. In these examples we see the classic form remaining constant, but reproduced in two widely differing sizes.

Variations on the covered jar are seen in the three examples in Plate

69D. Examples (*a*) and (*c*) are interesting for comparison with one another, the first having Waterford-type cutting and the latter Cork-type cutting, but both having turned-over rims. It is also interesting to contrast them with (*b*), for their bases are moulded whereas the base of (*b*) has rayed cuts beneath. The stem of (*a*) is not cut as it is in (*b*), and brings to mind the finial shanks on the covered urns of Plate 31. A Waterford provenance is suggested for this left-hand example, as it was for the urns.

The next covered jar (Plate 69A) is a curiosity. With its wide heavy handles, flat cover, moulded foot of unusual design, it does not conform to previous examples. Its only recognizable feature is the sprig and oval engraved garland, a familiar device but not associated with a particular factory. The vessel has a Belfast background, and, as in the case of the *I. Irwin* decanter in Plate 45C, it may be presumed that *Arthur Davidson*, which name is engraved upon it, was a local personage.

The two covered jars (Plate 69Ba, b), also from Belfast, show the same shaped vessel partially cut (*a*) and completely finished (*b*). Allowance will of course be made for the difference in height of the two pieces; inevitably some of the thickness of the cover of the vessel on the left will be removed when the cutting is done. But even allowing for this cutting-away, the left hand jar would be higher and the button finial would be smaller than on the finished object on the right. But it will be noted that the circular foot in both instances is already star-cut beneath, and the knops of both the stems have been cut with facets. The craftsman has drawn a pattern on the piece to the left which does not suggest he was planning a companion piece to the one on the right.

*Glasses*

The types of glass in general use in Ireland within our period are rummers, goblets, wine glasses, tumblers, toasting glasses, cordials, table glasses in sets; and syllabub, jelly, and wet and dry sweetmeat glasses.

'The word rummer is a corruption of the German Römer. . . . It has no connection with the spirit rum.'[1] As early as 1770 Williams of Dublin advertised rummers.[2] The glass in question had little of the character of its German forebear of a century or two earlier. In the late-eighteenth century it was an ample and sturdy vessel with an ovate bowl, perhaps with a bladed knop and a short stem leading to a circular or moulded foot. It might be decorated by cutting or engraving or by both.

[1] Thorpe, p. 326.          [2] Westropp, p. 57.

Four typical rummers are illustrated in Plates 70B, 70C, 70D, 71A. All are of late-eighteenth to early-nineteenth-century date. The bowl of the first is gracefully relieved in its plainness by leaf festoons and handsome stars, all cut very flat in *Cork Glass Co.* style. In the first example (Plate 70B), the base of the bowl has a handsome circlet of tapered flat cut flutes. As noted below, this tapered flat flute detail is observed also on vessels of the Down Hunt.

We return to *Cork Glass Co.* with the crosshatched vesica in the Plate 70D example, one of a pair, and to *Waterloo Co. Cork* with the bowknot and leaf-frond engraving on the vessel in Plate 71A.

The ovate rummer was also made in a modified form at approximately the same time as the preceding examples. Vessels with rounded or bucket type bowl and longer stem are seen in Plates 71B, 71C and 71D. All of them are engraved. The first follows the *Waterloo Co. Cork* bowknot prototype while the second, which is one of a set of seven, is engraved with more originality with a delicate circlet of leaves and trailing shamrock. The Down Hunt example (Plate 71D) is one of numerous pieces engraved with a shamrock device, another version of which was seen in Plate 44A.

The following four examples may be designated as either very elegant rummers of a later period, or as goblets. They are of approximately the same height as the rummers.

The first of the four (Plate 70A) has a bucket bowl. It was made in honour of the visit to Dublin of George IV in 1821; the engraving, in addition to G R IV, 1821, reads 'Caed Mille Failte (One Hundred Thousand Welcomes)'. As in the instance of the decanters in Plate 49A, in this goblet there are traces of oil gilding.

The three glasses in Plate 72A are obviously not of a set, but they have marked similarities and only minor differences other than their conspicuous difference in shape.

A Waterford attribution seems assured for the tumbler in Plate 73C. The columns and arches, both filled with fine diamonds and combined with cut stars and splits at the arch junctions, are all characteristic of *Penrose Waterford* (cf: Plates 11, 12, 13A).

The tumblers (*a*) and (*b*) of Plate 72B are attributed to Cork. For the former, reference is made to the marked example in Plate 9B; for the latter, to the *Cork Corporation* engraved example in Plate 75D.[1] Such glasses are uncommon whether with or without the foot. The rayed base of the Plate 73A example suggests a nineteenth-century date for it.

The mug in Plate 73D conforms admirably with loop handle, cut

[1] Vessels with notched rims are discussed in Appendix B.

thumb rest, band of sharp medium diamonds, wide flat flutes, to other Irish pieces. Its curved reserved areas, however, are unusual. It was acquired near Belfast.

The tumbler shown in Plate 73B, with a ship engraved on one side and on the other side with 'Succes To The/Speedwell/Capt McLelland', is attributed to Cork.

The last remaining tumbler (Plate 73E) is significant because its provenance may be so clearly established. It is engraved 'William Rex The III' and thus bears out a comment made earlier about the continuation of the hero-worship of William up to the late-eighteenth to early-nineteenth century. But in addition to being engraved with the figure of William, it is also engraved 'Orange Lodge/No, 60, July 12th/ 1690'. Now, while it is possible that a number forfeited by one lodge may be reassigned to another, and while early records on these matters were destroyed during the 1916–1921 troubles, the number 60 was originally allocated to the Lodge at Scarva, near Tandragee.[1] Scarva was the rendezvous for William's forces prior to the Boyne, and it has been the scene of sham fights held annually on July 13, commemorating the battle. On this vessel occur the ubiquitous bowknot and ribbon device, generally associated with *Waterloo Co. Cork* (opened 1815), a curious circumstance on a glass with an Ulster background. In this instance, however, it is more carefully rendered than on any of the marked *Waterloo Co. Cork* examples.

The first two of the three toasting glasses (Plates 76B, 76D) are Volunteer glasses and thus, in their decoration at least, essentially Irish. The third glass (Plate 76D) reflects the important role in Irish political history played by Sir George Ponsonby (1755–1817). Air-twist and opaque-twist stems, so much a speciality of the English glass houses in the middle of the eighteenth century and later, were apparently not much made in Ireland. It is probable, therefore, that the *Ireland For Ever* vessel (Plate 76B) and the *Ponsonby* glass (Plate 76D) are English pieces engraved in Ireland. The 'Loyal Dublin Artillery/The/Goldsmiths Company' glass, however, is most likely of Irish origin. As glasses, none of these examples have any outstanding Irish characteristics: with their engraved inscriptions, however, they do indeed reflect the fervour of a significant moment in the turbulent history of Ireland.

In Plate 76A are shown three of an existing set of four cordial glasses,

[1] The writer acknowledges his indebtedness to Mr. Wilfred A. Seaby, Director of the Ulster Museum, Belfast, for this interesting reference.

sometimes called dram or spirit glasses. By contrast with the preceding toasting glasses, which were uniformly about 6″ high, these cordials are only 3¾ in. high. Because of the thickened bases of the bucket bowls, the vessels are probably of about the same capacity as the toasting glasses. But, again in contrast to the Volunteer glasses with their cannon and piles of shot, these are engraved with the pacific symbols of the Union of 1800, the rose, the thistle and the shamrock. But these small glasses have an Ulster provenance and it may be they belong to that family of glasses 'swiftly and inexpensively made', and exported from Belfast according to Customs House records. Engraving, however, would most probably be omitted on the export product.

A glass which relates in shape to previous examples, notably the com-memorative George IV example (Plate 70A), is the mixing glass inscribed *Cork Corporation* (Plate 75D). This vessel has several most unusual characteristics. Lipped vessels, with and without feet, are occasionally to be seen (cf. Plates 72B, 73A) but they are rarely as large as this mixing glass. The inscription effectively indicates its provenance. The com-bination of this inscription with the band of fine diamonds supports the claim to Cork origin of pieces such as the miniature piggin (Plate 81A), the Penrose flask (Plates 83A, 83B), the tumbler (Plate 72B*b*), all probably late-eighteenth-century vessels.

Earlier in this chapter reference was made to table glass in sets. We now come to three sets, two of which have Irish family histories. Further, the second and third of the sets may be attributed to specific factories.

The examples in the first set (Plate 74A) are from the family collection of the late Captain Alfred Grahame MacMullen. It will be recalled that Captain MacMullen was a descendant of the Penroses, Elizabeth Penrose (married to Anthony Robinson of Moate, 1805) being his great grand mother. This Robinson connexion is important because several of the glasses in the MacMullen collection carry initials of Robinson family members. Examples (*b*) and (*c*) of Plate 74A, are initialled A R for Anthony Robinson, and T R for another Robinson.[1]

It will be seen that examples (*a*) and (*d*) are similar in shape but of different size, that they have hexagonal cut stems and identical engraved decoration. The vessels with the initial R have engraving which is in part

---

[1] In addition to the A R tumbler, 2¾ in. high, which is one of two remaining, there is a W H R tumbler of identical size; while in addition to the T R wine (also 2¾ in. high), there are numerous other wines initialled P R and W H R.

similar to, but not identical with, the uninitialled pieces. Very probably we have here examples of two sets, made at different times, possibly for two generations, and possibly by different glass houses.

Notwithstanding the MacMullen-Penrose-Waterford connexion, there are no features of the R glasses which suggest a Waterford attribution. The character of the engraving suggests a Cork origin; the Robinsons, being a Westmeath family (Moate is virtually in the centre of Ireland), might readily have acquired this glass on a venture from Cork or from a Dublin outlet for the Cork factory.

The Robinsons' daughter, however, Susannah Penrose Robinson, Captain MacMullen's grandmother, married a MacMullen of Cork. The uninitialled vessels may have come down from this later generation, a theory their late shape would support.[1] This would imply a Waterloo origin for them before 1835, when Waterloo ceased operations.

With regard to the set of glasses in Plate 74B from the collection of the Rev. Mr. R. M. L. Westropp, the character of the engraving strongly indicates the *Cork Glass Co.* We hardly need to know that this glass 'has always been in the family' and that the Westropps were Cork people. In the set there are very many pieces remaining, naturally more of some types than of others. It is an interesting detail that the comb flutes of the finger bowl are cut, not moulded. Since the *Cork Glass Co.* went out of business permanently in 1818, these examples of their work must antedate that year.

A very large number of glasses and finger bowls (e.g., 20 of the latter), of various sizes and types, remain from the set of table glass in Plate 75A belonging to the Marquess of Bute. Because of their high quality of metal and cutting, the wide band of medium plain diamonds, and the numerous examples of similar shapes seen in the Miller patterns, these glasses and finger bowls warrant a Waterford attribution.

### Dry and Wet Sweetmeats

Sweetmeat glasses belong to the dessert services of numerous advertisements in Irish newspapers of the eighteenth century. Because desserts included both dry sweetmeats (e.g., sugared chips of citrus peel, ginger, chocolates, bonbons, almonds, etc.), and wet sweetmeats (creams, syllabubs, jellies, custards, semi-liquid confections consumed with a spoon), glasses of different character came into use.[2]

[1] It has been pointed out to the writer that the ogee curved or bell-shaped profile as seen in examples (*a*) and (*d*) of Plate 74A is to be noted in English work of the 1830's and 1840's (cf. Wakefield, p. 21, Plates 50A and 50B).

[2] I believe that Thorpe has unintentionally reversed the order of the use of these vessels, in placing the wet sweet meats in the tall open topped vase and the dry ones in the smaller glasses with short stems or no stems at all.

D. Gilded plate with painted Drogheda crest. Diameter $7\frac{1}{4}$ in. Attributed to John Grahl, Dublin. *c.* 1786. Courtesy of the Victoria and Albert Museum. (See page 114)

Typical dry sweetmeat glasses are tall, stemmed vessels, with capacious bowls sometimes flaring and generally with cut rims, on spreading round feet usually plain but sometimes petalled. The bowls may carry flat cutting, and if the rims have pronounced trefoil cutting the articles may well be of Irish origin. Such vessels were made in Ireland prior to 1800. After that date they appear to have been replaced by covered jars or later by comports which doubled as pedestalled serving-bowls. Today Irish standing sweetmeats are infrequently found.[1]

On the other hand there is no dearth of vessels suitable for wet sweetmeats and the examples in Plate 75B are a selection which could be expanded almost indefinitely; the profusion in which such glasses were made is equalled only by the variety. Many of the characteristics of design and cutting observed in Irish glass thus far described will be seen here again. Of particular note are two custard glasses: (*a*) one of a pair, with upstanding rim of short flutes and conical cover (notched for a protruding spoon), with button finial; and (*e*) which is one of many matching cups, and has a remarkable number and combination of familiar cutting motifs for so small an object.[2]

The affinity of the punch cup on Plate 75C with the *Cork Corporation* mixing glass (Plate 75D) will be noted.

*Plates*

The Irish glass plate, commonly called a dessert plate, shares with the glass serving plate the characteristic of a wide horizontal flange or rim. It is also apt to be thin of metal, therefore fragile, which no doubt accounts for its limited survival; single glass plates are rare, sets of six or a dozen seldom encountered. In cases where the flange or rim is rolled over and not horizontally extended, the possibility exists of mistaking plates for stands of missing bowls; stands, however, are inclined to be thicker in section than plates. The dimensions of the dish shown in Plate 77B may be taken as average: diameter overall, $7\frac{3}{4}$ in.; flange from

[1] An example of a stemmed sweetmeat glass having the characteristics mentioned above, notably the Van Dyck cut rim, is illustrated in Thorpe, Plate CVII, 3.

[2] Apropos of vessels for sweetmeats, mention should be made of another type, an all glass epergne, a splendid example of which was in the Bles Collection. From a vase shaft, which arose from a heavy, moulded foot (as shown in Plate 39A), there extended six notched branches each terminating in an attached saucer. Rising supreme from the centre of all this was a bowl. The bowl, the saucers and the central vase were all richly ornamented with flat cutting. The piece is illustrated in Hughes, no. 235, facing p. 292, described p. 300.

edge to cavetto, 1 in.; height at rim, 1 in. Two exceptions to these average dimensions are shown (Colour Plate D and the saucer in Plate 77A). The first, the gilded dish of Colour Plate D, has a diameter of $7\frac{1}{4}$ in., but at least two sizes of this same dish are known to have been made.[1] The dish shown carries the moor's head in profile, couped at the shoulder, banded argent and gules above a coronet, flanked with laurel wreaths, which is the crest of the Drogheda family (cf. Plate 26). It will be recalled that Charles Moore, of a family long identified with Irish history, was created Marquess of Drogheda in the Irish peerage in 1781. In the centre of the dish is a spray of red currants and a butterfly. Hitherto several instances have been noted of traces of oil gilding remaining in engraved monograms or mottoes (e.g., Plate 49A). These Drogheda plates, however, are among the very rare Irish objects to be wholly gilded and may be considered most exceptional.

They are attributed to a German named John Grahl, who is believed to have come from Saxony. In 1785 he sought the support of the Royal Dublin Society, exhibiting glass 'curiously gilt'. The dearth today of gilded glass of Irish provenance suggests that Grahl did not flourish in his gilding practice.

The second exception to the rule of thumb regarding the size of Irish glass plates occurs on the quite rare dish shown in Plate 77A, which is only about the size of a saucer. It is very thick. It may have been used beneath a sweetmeat glass. It has the deeply cut prismatic band also evident in Colour Plate D.

The glass plate shown in Plate 77B is one of a half-dozen. Attention is drawn to the prismatic cutting on the underside of the floor of this example, a treatment noticed in the boat-shaped bowl in Plate 65B. Use of prismatic cutting on flat surfaces is less usual than on convex vessels (cf. Plates 55C, 68C).

The dish in Plate 77E belongs to the Corporation of Waterford Service and is notable for the double drapery swags filled with fine diamonds, and the dramatic type of cut star which radiates from a petalled centre on the underside of the plate. This very bold treatment of the plate centre is most unusual.[2]

Rayed cutting in different styles is illustrated in the plates in Plates

[1] The glass plate shown is illustrated in two sizes, but without dimensions being given, in the Walter Harding Collection Catalogue (see Bibliography), p. 43, described as 'Set of Three Small and Three Large . . . Plates'. In addition to the example shown in Colour Plate D, another one of the former set of six may be seen at the Cecil Higgins Art Gallery, Bedford.

[2] It is strongly reminiscent of pictorial wood inlays on fine cabinet work of the period.

77D, 77C, 77E. The combination of rayed flutes and the circle of flutes within the rim of the example in Plate 77D should be noted. The eight petals of the flower cut into the base of the plate in 77C are filled with fine diamonds and recall George W. Penrose's glass flask (Plates 83A, 83B).

## Cream Jugs

A useful comparison may be made between the cream jug (Plate 78A*a*) and the covered urns in Plate 29. On the low cream jug there are the identical cutting devices which were so effectively used to produce a limpid quality on the high urns. On the jug they are simply reduced in number and in scale. The profile of the rim reflects that of the jugs in Plate 54A*a*, *b*. This cream jug has a slightly blue cast, a characteristic which was also noted in the covered urns referred to above.

The cream jug in Plate 78A*b* is of an absolutely colourless metal and it is notable for two reasons. First, the rim is turned in, providing an interior flange the top surface of which is cut with short flutes, a detail which will be noted again below as a characteristic of late, ball-shaped salts. Perhaps because it effectively obviates slopping of the vessel's contents, cream jugs with this feature have been dubbed 'yacht jugs'. The second notable detail about this jug is the perfectly proportioned and executed star cut within the equally fine, flat ovals on the sides of the piece. A precision in cutting was achieved here which was not matched in a somewhat similar treatment shown on the bowl in Plate 63B.

## Salts

Within the period salts are of two rather clearly defined types. These are shown in chronological order in Plates 78B–79C inclusive. An interpretation of the classic oval bowl is the earlier of the two types, and the examples illustrated in Plates 78B and 78C may be considered typical. It will be noted that the foot is a lozenge in one instance, an oval in another. The former is cut, the latter moulded. The lozenge base is solid, the oval base is of the domed 'lemon-squeezer' variety. Circular salts on stems with circular bases also occur at this period and stemmed salts with turned-over rim and modest cutting, reminiscent of bowls of a much larger size, are also to be seen. All these salts are of the late eighteenth–early nineteenth century.

As the Age of Exuberance progresses, the salt-cellar loses its pedestal foot and its neo-classic oval bowl, and becomes nearly ball-shaped, open on top. The opening may be cut in scallops, as in the example seen in Plate 78D, or the rim may be turned in, providing the same interior flange as noted on the cream jug (Plate 78Ab), and seen to good advantage in the salt shown in Plate 78E. This picture also shows the top surface of the flange cut with a band of short flutes. This flange detail is repeated in still another pair of salts shown in Plate 88Ba, d, as part of the Wadsworth Atheneum Service.

In Plate 79C is an open salt, of interest because it combines the turned-over rim with a notable wealth of cutting.

The octagonal saucer seen in Plate 79D may well be a late salt or it may be a fitting from an epergne. It clearly illustrates the cutting device known as crosscut diamonds. This is a type of cutting found toward the end of the Age of Exuberance. Inasmuch as it falls within the international style, the Irishness of pieces so cut cannot be assumed as readily as with pieces like the open salt and earlier examples which are cut with devices more characteristically Irish.

### Sifters

Whether they are called sifters or casters, all the vessels pictured in Plate 80B were made with a uniform purpose – the sprinkling of flavourings on food. Example (*a*) has a removable Sheffield plate top (its silver base may be a replacement); otherwise, each vessel is complete in itself with no detachable parts. This includes the example (*c*), the covered urn, which, most surprisingly, is made in one piece. Except for example (*a*), all vessels are filled through corked openings beneath.

The five pieces present a very wide range of cutting styles which over and over again in this study have been identified as essentially Irish. One may point out the comparatively early flat cutting in example (*d*), which contributes to the frequently mentioned limpid quality of glass associated with Cork; also the exuberance achieved in example (*c*) with its repertoire of cutting devices; the rim of short vertical flutes on example (*e*) is the same motif, upside down, as may be seen in Plate 68E, a covered jar, and again in Plate 34C, a pair of candleholders. The triple drapery swags filled with fine flutes in example (*a*) have been so frequently observed heretofore that further comment upon their Irishness seems unnecessary.

### Cruets

The cruet bottle falls into a category related to the sifter. It was created to contain flavourings which were added to food and used at the table during meals. Very splendid cruet bottles with silver caps are shown in the centrepiece illustrated in Plate 27B and separately in Plate 27A. An assortment of vessels of a less pretentious nature but with typical Irish cutting, are shown in Plate 80A*b*, *c*, *d*. Each of the three bottles may have had from one to five mates, and the set of two to six bottles might have been held in a 'stand in silver or plated ware' with central carrying handle.

Also intended to contain flavouring ingredients is the covered pot (Plate 80A*a*) with its loop handle and fine diamond filled panels separated by herring-bone blazes. The jug (Plate 80A*e*) is a scaled down claret ewer with swan neck handle.

### Piggins

The piggin is essentially an Irish vessel; it does not appear that it was ever made in England. It is described in the dictionary as 'a small pail or cylindrical vessel, esp. a wooden one with one stave longer than the rest serving as a handle; a milking pail; a vessel to drink out of'. While its origin may have been humble, in the Age of Exuberance it achieved in the medium of cut glass a notable degree of magnificence, as is shown in Plates 79A, 79B.[1]

### (c) Miscellaneous

### Miniatures

Miniatures occupy an interesting but minor place in the history of Irish glass in our period. They often illustrate by their careful workmanship a serious purpose which dissociates them from toys.

The two bowls shown in Plates 81B and 81C are too large to be salts, although it is not obvious what their use was. The latter example has a typically Irish moulded hollow base and its alternate prisms and large hollow facet cutting may be compared to the same motifs seen in Plates 41C, 41E.

The jug in Plate 81D (cf. Plate 59A) is, in turn, remarkable for its small size. Notable also are the two bands of trailed threads encircling the body of the jug.

[1] The piece shown on Plate 79A was included in the Walter Harding Collection Catalogue (see Bibliography) and was described as a whipped cream pail; ill. p. 69, description, p. 44.

The piggin in Plate 81A is broader than it is high. The cutting on it is very delicate and very flat, although the thickness in section of the piggin does not require this flatness. On the strength of previous examples with these attributes it is difficult not to associate this piece with Cork. Its colour is slightly blue.

### Scent-bottles (*Vials*)

The three following pieces (Plates 82C, 82D, 82A, 82B) and similar vessels are usually termed 'scent-bottles' today, but the term 'vial' which occurs in Irish newspaper advertisements describes them more accurately; the scent-bottle properly so-called will be seen in Plate 84Ca,c. Vials usually are flat and have tiny glass stoppers which are enclosed by a screw-on silver cap.

All three of the examples shown have Waterford Glass House connexions. That of the first (Plate 82C), inscribed 'L'Amitie/Vous L'Offre/Waterford/Feb[ry] T[H] 15/1794', with the initials TB, is obvious. For the Waterford connexion of the next (Plate 82D), we must recall Susannah Gatchell, sister of Jonathan Gatchell (1752–1823), who married Nehemiah Wright and was the mother of Jonathan, John and Nathan Wright, all of whom played such important rôles in Waterford Glass House history. Susannah Gatchell's perfume vial, identified by the initials SG, is pictured in Plate 82D. This vial was formerly the property of Samuel Hudson Wright (see p. 41).

We extend even further back into Waterford Glass House history, however, with the vial shown in Plates 82A, B, which has been handed down through generations of Penrose descendants. It is initialed RP and SE, the former initials being for Rachel Nevins Penrose, wife of William Penrose, one of the two Waterford Glass House founders.[1] This is a memorial vessel, for on the side with the RP is inscribed 'Look And Remember' while on the SE side are the words 'Dearly Beloved'. There are, also, long fronds embracing the initials and inscriptions; engraved flowers (after the style on flowered decanters); and, most curiously of all, a typical *Waterloo Co. Cork* bowknot and ribbon decoration.

Inevitably one must speculate as to why a vessel so identified with a member of the Waterford family of Penrose should be engraved with a design so closely associated with a Cork glass house. It will be recalled, however, that there were Penrose family members who lived in Cork, and that there is still a Penrose Quay in Cork. The bottle need not be of Waterford make; it might just as readily have been made and sent by

---

[1] Unfortunately the identity of SE is unknown.

SE in Cork to Rachel Penrose in Waterford as the other way around. In itself, this bottle is a most thought-provoking and interesting piece, especially when compared with the bottles of assured Waterford provenance which preceded it in this account.

## Scent Bottles

Scent *bottles* (Plate 84Ca, *c*), in contrast to the preceding *vials*, are seen in two examples which demonstrate to advantage several cutting techniques, *viz*: Waterford-style pillar flutes alternating with panels of fine diamonds; a broad field of sharp medium diamonds, and cut mushroom stoppers.

## Hyacinth Vases

Vessels for growing bulbs, called 'bulb', 'hyacinth' or 'flower root' glasses, are seen in Plates 84C and 85A. The first example is interesting because, coincidentally, it exactly matches in profile, although not in cutting, a specimen belonging in 1920 in the collection of Lady Moore, Dublin.[1] Although the vessels are thick in section, in both cases their cutting is of the flat variety characteristic of Cork. The example with the wide bands of meticulously executed sharp diamonds (Plate 84C*b*) is of somewhat later date than the preceding one.

## Flasks

Two Irish glass flasks, probably originally encased in leather holsters and attached to saddles, are shown in Plates 83A, 83B, 83C.

The latter is simply but expertly cut on both sides with a giant star, rendered very flat. The restraint in the cutting of this piece proposes a date earlier than that under which it was catalogued at one time ('c. 1815').[2]

Of commanding interest is the flask shown in two views (Plates 83A, 83B). This piece is unique in being engraved with the initials of George W. Penrose.

The bottle in Plates 84A, 84B, is attributed to Belfast on the strength of its engraved names 'Watts Carrick/Fergus', the latter being a port town

[1] Westropp, illustrated Plate II, bottom, r, facing p. 22.
[2] Walter Harding Collection Catalogue (see Bibliography), ill. p. 55, described p. 40.

once of importance, on Belfast Lough, Co. Antrim, about ten miles from Belfast.[1] Sometimes called a 'gemel' bottle, a vessel of this type is composed of twin flattened pear shaped flasks, separately blown and fused together with the spouts turned to right and left. While probably intended as a souvenir, commemorative or presentation piece, it might have served for oil and vinegar or for two kinds of liquor. Trailed decoration has been used as an important decorative feature.

A similar double bottle, engraved with a harp and a shamrock leaf crown, attributed to Belfast and dated to the early nineteenth century is known.[2] No inference is here intended that the double bottle was a speciality of the Belfast glass houses; the writer has also seen several such bottles in a private collection in Cork and they were all bought in that city. While not attributable to a specific Irish city or factory, it is clear that such bottles were indigenous to Ireland.

*Toddy-lifters*

As seen in Plate 85B*a*, *b*, *c*, the toddy-lifter is a bulb-shaped vessel with a long neck whose very practical use is exactly explained in its name. It is open at both ends. To use it, you plunged the bulb section into a bowl or mixing glass similar to the *Cork Corporation* example (Plate 75D). You allowed the bulb to fill, then captured the contents by placing a finger tip over the hole in the top, thus creating a vacuum. The next step was to withdraw the bulb from the punch bowl, hold it over a glass, and, by removing the finger from the hole in the stem top, to allow the imprisoned liquid to flow out.

Very probably toddy-lifters, being objects of minor importance, were included in phrases such as 'every other article in the glass way' or 'flint glass of every description', in glass house advertisements. Unfortunately, no toddy-lifter with Penrose or Gatchell associations has come to light, and one would hesitate to affirm more with regard to the three examples than that they all display the cutting motifs already associated with glass of assured Irish origin.

*Linen-Smoother*

Another object of very probable but unconfirmed Irish provenance is the linen-smoother (Plate 85C*a*). Such utensils were in general use but

---

[1] It was at Carrickfergus that William III landed on June 14, 1690, with his united force of 36,000 mercenaries, prior to the Battle of the Boyne.

[2] Westropp. Plate XL, facing p. 198.

because of their simplicity of design and lack of decoration they provide minimal grounds for attribution.

## Bowl-stand

The object shown in Plate 85c*b* is a stand for a bowl which is missing; a somewhat similar stand will be seen under the bowl with turned-over rim in the Wellington Service (Plate 91A). Such bowl-stands are not to be confused with the well-known rings of silver or Sheffield plate mentioned in Chapter 8(*a*), although the glass stands have the same general shape as the silver equivalents.[1] The stand in Plate 85c*b* is cut with familiar Irish motifs.

## Hookah-base

In Plate 86B is illustrated a vase for the water of a hookah. This is a Middle Eastern smoking device, completed by a flexible tube by means of which smoke is drawn through the water and into the smoker's mouth.

The Irish Custom House export records do not specifically mention Middle Eastern ports as ports of destination, but unquestionably Irish glass hookah-bases were made to supply an export market in the eastern Mediterranean and in India. Many bases, some even taller than this one, may be seen in the museum of the Topkapi Sarayi in Istanbul.

The example in Plate 86B is of exceptionally clear glass. The cutting of its sharp plain diamonds, prismatic rings and several types of flutes, is so clean and exact that the hookah measures up to Waterford Glass House standards.[2]

## Mirrors

The example in Plate 86A may be taken as a typical though modest

[1] *Antiques*, March, 1950, p. 191, article: Irish Domestic Silver by Kirt Ticher: 'Probably the best-known of all typically Irish silver objects is the dish ring, wrongly called the Potato Ring.'

[2] In connexion with hookahs, I am indebted to Robert J. Charleston for reminding me of John Blades of London, in an illustration of whose London showroom of the 1780's numerous hookahs appear. Blades was a figure of importance in the field of glass, as indicated by his being called in 1783 to testify about English–Irish commercial relations to a Committee of Enquiry; his report on that occasion about John Hill's having gone from Worcester to Waterford indicates his familiarity with the Waterford Glass House, from where the hookahs in his showroom may have been imported, either as blanks for Blades' own cutting or as finished Waterford vessels. Hookahs require a quantity of metal which may bespeak their Irish origin.

example of Irish looking-glasses of the period. Variations of this type are many and often most elaborate.

A first variation lies in size: the mirror shown is small but mirrors of this type, while remaining oval in shape, are seen half as large again or even larger.

A second major variation is provided by the facetted glass 'jewels', cut as flat diamonds and set into a lead channel encircling the glass. In the mirror shown all 'jewels' are clear, but mirrors are sometimes found with facetted components which are all blue, or opaque, or green, or in combinations of these colours: that is, a few clear 'jewels' next to one another, alternating with a few blue ones, or the same with green 'jewels', etc. Red 'jewels' have been noted also. Occasionally there will be several bands of 'jewels', the outer ones perhaps all clear, the inner ones alternating in coloured pairs. Sometimes the 'jewels', instead of being diamond facetted, are cut with two or three parallel flutes and in some examples these flutes have been gilded. Finally, another variation is when the mirror is used as a background for a chandelier suspended from above; then the canopies, arms, prisms, etc., of the hanging fixture are doubled by reflection.

*Hanging Lamp*

'Fine large globe lamps for halls' happen to occupy first place in the lists already quoted of the types of glass most frequently advertised in late-eighteenth to early-nineteenth-century newspapers. Such advertisements occurred as early as 1784. Apparently made in quantity, the globes were exported to a wide market; they have appeared in the Orient and also in the United States, where they were widely copied. They were made to accommodate from one to four candles.

With its waisted profile, the lamp in Plate 86c is a late interpretation of the tall, slim globe which protected from draughts the candles in wall or ceiling fixtures in halls and stairwells of Georgian houses. It may be considered typical of its kind: numerous cutting motifs characteristic of Irish glass of the period will be noted. The essential Irishness of this type of globe is affirmed in the correspondence which constitutes Appendix G (An Historical Note on the Marquess of Bute's Collection).

Another type of hanging fixture in the design of which a single piece of Irish glass plays a predominant part is composed of a circular dish of varying depth, perhaps 18 in. diameter, flat cut on its underside with bands of blazes, printies, etc., and with the rim in a very bold trefoil cut or a version thereof, or edged with a metal frame. Mounted above this single piece of glass, which was suspended by chains, were as many as four metal reservoirs or fonts for the fuel, which was thus fed by gravity (in contrast to being drawn up by a wick).[1]

This type of glass fixture, with its oil fuel replacing the candle, was a later style of fixture than the hanging globe in Plate 86c.[2]

[1] In a series of drawing rooms and hall passages in a residence in Berkshire there are a half dozen such hanging lamps, now converted to electricity. The large circular plates have marked Irish characteristics; they were installed about 1817, and the original owner of the mansion had strong Irish affiliations.

Several variations of chandeliers of this late type are illustrated in *Duncan Phyfe & the English Regency*, McClelland, New York, 1939. The best illustrations are Plate 42, Regency Room from Buckingham Palace, and Plate 39, Entrance Hall, Holme House, Regent's Park.

[2] The so-called 'Waterford' chandelier and related table and wall lighting devices are discussed in Appendix E.

# 9

# Services

## General

Eighteenth-century Irish newspaper advertisements for glass services probably referred to services for desserts, and might have included sweet-meat glasses, jelly glasses, plates, salvers, saucers, even epergnes, for these were part of the dessert equipment, and were frequently accorded separate listings in advertisements. There appear to have been no single meaning for the term dessert service or exact specifications for its composition. The expression was used at least until 1835, when it appears in an advertisement for the Ronaynes' Terrace Glass Works in Cork.

On occasion in the advertisements the term 'service' is qualified by the adjective 'military'. We may recall the handsomely engraved 'Royal Dublin Infantry' finger bowl impressed with the name of *Francis Collins Dublin* (Plate 20B) to which a late-eighteenth-century date was ascribed. Another instance of the military being interested in Irish glass is the Waterford Glass House bookkeeping entry for the year 1816: 'Mess of the 16th Regiment supplied with glass L. £44.0.10'.[1] Unfortunately, the record yields no list of what constituted a military service. Most likely, when it was intended for officers' messes, it included glasses in various sizes, also finger bowls. The presence of finger bowls for the officers' tables need not surprise us if we reflect that the finger bowl was a multi-purpose vessel (Appendix C).

A news item from the *Dublin Chronicle* for Saturday, August 23, 1788, is of importance in connexion with this subject of services. It relates that 'A very curious service of glass has been sent over from Waterford to Milford for their Majesties' use, and by their orders forwarded to Cheltenham, where it has been much admired, and does great credit to the manufacture of this country.' In this notice there is a first formal acknowledgement of Waterford's involvement in the making of glass services, an involvement on a Royal level and deserving a news item in the Dublin paper. Unfortunately, no record of this service, giving

[1] Westropp, p. 87.

details of either its composition or its destiny, has come to light in the Royal Archives.[1]

In the year 1837, when Terrace Glass Works offered 'Military services of glass engraved to order or pattern',[2] another Irish advertisement offered '*sets* of glassware'. At that time the term *service* would perhaps have been reserved for a wider assortment of articles than a *set* would include. A service assortment might have included serving bowls, ewers, comports, etc., all cut with an identical pattern just as porcelain services were painted with identical patterns or related subject matter.

It should be stressed that unlike collectors' items today, acquired for cabinet display, services, especially family services, were bought for use. During the past 150 years, such services have indeed been used; they have, perhaps, been more subject to use than to love; they have been destroyed through breakage, and they have been subjected to division among family members. For these reasons their survival today in any degree of completeness is all the more remarkable. It is hoped that the focusing of attention on four surviving services may prompt owners of other services to take stock of their treasures. It is time the glass service of the early 1800's came out of the butler's pantry and found its rightful place in a proper cabinet, to be seen, enjoyed and used on occasion, and cherished.

### (a) The Wadsworth Atheneum Service[3]

As mentioned in Chapter 8, prismatic cutting was extensively employed in Ireland after Free Trade and it reached the zenith of its Irish popu-

[1] An interesting sidelight on this matter, although it concerns English and not Irish glass, is a bill of sale to the Prince of Wales, the future George IV, dated December, 1807, a copy of which has been furnished by gracious permission of the Queen from the Royal Archives, Windsor, by Mr. Robert Mackworth-Young, the Librarian. On a bill-head of John and James Davenport. Potters and Glass Makers, Longport, near Newcastle, Staffordshire, the following entry for April 18 appears:

A Service of Glass Etch[d] Grecian border, as under:
48 Montieths (*sic*), 72 Wine & Water Glasses, 24 Ale Glasses, 60 Wine Glasses, 24 Liquor Glasses, 6 Quart Decanters & Stoppers Etch[d] Feathers, 6 Thumbprint Water Carafes, 6 Quart double ring[d] Decanters Etch[d] 6 Quart Decanters richly cutt & Etch[d] His Royal Highness Arms in full.

[2] Westropp, p. 126.

[3] The service was acquired by the Wadsworth Atheneum of Hartford, Connecticut, in 1957, by gift of Miss Ellen A. Jarvis, a collateral descendant of Captain Isaac Hull to whom it once belonged. Captain Hull will be remembered as the commander of the United States frigate *Constitution* which, on the nineteenth of August, 1812, vanquished the British frigate *Guerrière*, Captain James Richard Dacres, commanding.

larity in the early decades of the nineteenth century. Its use cannot be ascribed to a particular Irish glass house; while associated with Waterford, it is not a 'signature' of Waterford to the extent that pillar flutes are, for example. But because prismatic cutting requires the best of metal for its effect, pieces which are superior in both their metal and prismatic cut craftsmanship are generally ascribed to the Waterford Glass House.

The Atheneum service is composed of over eighty pieces divided between 14 different types of vessel, and all of the pieces are completely decorated with prismatic cutting. Scrutiny of the Plates 87A–C, 88A–B, will reveal many details which attest the service's Irishness. These details include the swan-neck handle of the ewer; this tapered and clipped handle is very similar to the handle seen on the spouted jug of Plate 54B ascribed to Waterford partially because of the pillar flute cutting on its body. The facetted shanks of the mushroom stoppers are seen again on the ewers in Plate 55C and on the 'Old Bushmills' decanter in Plate 46A. Both the plate, with its minimal area for use and its wide flat flange, and the serving bowls, have the by now familiar bold cutting beneath. The rims of the serving bowls repeat with their flutes the vertical flute edging seen on the covers and bodies of covered urns. Also to be noted is the opening of the salts, the way the rim is cut in short flutes which extend into and over the interior of the vessel as in the yacht jug shown in Plate 78A*b* and on the salt in Plate 78E.

The depth of the prismatic cutting on the sides of the salts and on the oval bowl in the Atheneum service reveals the amount of metal which was cut away.

The surviving serving-bowls are eight in number, the three sizes ranging down from a maximum length of $10\frac{3}{4}$ in. There are two oval bowls with their matching stands. The dramatic ear-handles are deeply cut and fan shaped, as normally they may be expected to be. But the fact that they are flattened to carry outward to left and right the movement of the slanted sides of the bowl gives them a highly individual appearance. There are precedents for the sloping sides of the flat-based bowls (tripod bowl, Plate 40A; two eared bowl, Plate 90B), but the flattened handles are not common to Irish work.

The decanters, it will be noted, are in two sizes. Their stoppers are identical, and probably original since they are four in number and the likelihood of their being other than original is slight.

There are 16 large wine-glasses (height $4\frac{5}{8}$ in.) and 15 small ones (height $4\frac{1}{4}$ in.). In these numbers there is perhaps a hint that the wine glasses are later additions to the service. They do not have quite the solidity of the other pieces and the number surviving further arouses the suspicion that they may have been added.

The possessions of colourful personalities often acquire colourful legends, and the Wadsworth Atheneum service, once the property of the renowned Captain Hull, is no exception.

The legend exists that the service was seized by Captain Hull in 1812 after the *Constitution-Guerrière* engagement and taken aboard the *Constitution* before Hull caused the *Guerrière* to be burned because she was 'not worth towing into Port'.[1]

This tradition is supported by the known fact that Captain Hull *did* seize the *Guerrière*'s flag and retain it as a personal memento of his victory.[2] He did not surrender it until invited to do so in a hand-written letter from the Secretary of the Navy dated October 21, 1812, in which the Secretary referred to the flag as a 'highly precious' national trophy.

The tradition of the glass service's having been seized from the *Guerrière* is strengthened by the fact that, in addition to the flag, Captain Hull seized from the defeated ship two oil paintings. 'Before destroying her, he sent an officer on board to secure something from her as a relic, and he, the officer, cut from the panels of the captain's cabin these paintings'.[2] The paintings thus acquired Captain Hull presented to his sister-in-law, Mrs. Levi Hull. Her grandson, Dr. Isaac Hull Platt, gave them to the United States Navy Department in 1909. Dr. Platt, a prominent Philadelphian, accompanied his gift with a written statement to the effect that the panels had had but one owner between Captain Hull and himself – his grandmother. The paintings are today attributed to Claude Lorraine.[3]

In the presence of these facts, it is easy to comprehend the growth of the tradition concerning the provenance of the glass service.

It may seem surprising that the *Guerrière* would yield so splendid a prize and one so alien to the purpose of a frigate carrying 48 guns. But although the *Guerrière* has been described as old and worn out, there is no reason to suppose her captain while at sea would live in any less imposing a style than was customary for naval officers of the time. James Richard Dacres, commanding the *Guerrière*, was both the son and the

[1] Captain Hull's report from 'Off Boston Light August 30th. 1812, To the Hon.ble Paul Hamilton, Secretary of the Navy, Washington.' For a copy of this report and much other valuable historical information, the author acknowledges his debt to the office of the Director of Naval History, Department of the Navy, Washington.

[2] *History of Paintings from Panels of the Guerrière*, by Isaac Hull Platt, Wallingford, Penna., August 20, 1909, as supplied to the Superintendent, Library and Naval War Records, Navy Department, Washington.

[3] Correspondence, Author's files.

nephew of vice-admirals.[1] By the date of the engagement with 'Old Ironsides' he had been in command of the *Guerrière*'s 244 men for fifteen months. In providing handsomely for himself whilst at sea, Captain Dacres would have been following both the practice of the period and the distinguished precedent of the hero of Trafalgar, of whom it has been written that at his table aboard H.M.S. *Victory* he would *customarily* entertain ten or twelve persons.

Although the *Guerrière* emerged from her last engagement 'quite ungovernable', in 'shattered condition',[2] it may not be assumed that all her equipment below decks was destroyed. There had been ample time before the battle was joined for clearing for action. There would also have been time, after the action, for Captain Hull to have ordered the seizure of the Dacres glass, for the record is clear that he did order the seizure of the flag and the removal of the two oil paintings.

While it is impossible to be more specific than to suggest the first quarter of the nineteenth century as the probable date of the service, Captain Dacres' ownership of it in 1812 very comfortably fits into that twenty-five-year period.

While discretion dictates caution in assessing the colourful legend of the Atheneum's service, reasoned doubt about the legend does not affect the likelihood of the service's Irish origin, reduce its size or diminish its splendour.

### (b) The Service of the Corporation of Waterford[3]

The service displayed in the Council Chamber in Waterford's City Hall epitomises not only Irish glass in general but Waterford glass in particular, in characteristics which have been repeatedly observed in text and pictures throughout this study. It consists of fifty pieces and includes a covered urn (Plate 89B), three eared bowls with stands (Plate 90B), four waisted bowls with stands (Plate 90A), two bowls with both domed covers and stands (Plate 89A), twenty-four plates (Plate 77E), and, not illustrated, two large oval dishes and three round ones.

While the service is not as large in number of pieces as the Wadsworth Atheneum one, except for the Atheneum's eared oval bowl (Plate 88B), the Waterford service presents an array of more highly individual

[1] *A Naval Biographical Dictionary*, William R. O'Bryne, London, 1849, pp. 256–257.
[2] ibid.
[3] The service was presented to the Corporation of the City in September, 1964, by Edward A. McGuire, at that time Senator.

shapes. These include, of course, the urn, the eared bowls,[1] the waisted bowls and the dome-covered dish with stand. While these are remarkable pieces in themselves, it is the cutting which is especially notable and provides the irrefutable Waterford Glass House attribution.

The swag and fine diamonds, the most obvious of the service's 'hall marks', are abundantly evident, on both the cover and base of the urn, the domed cover, the ice pail and waisted bowl and all their stands as well. Even the plates, to the number of two dozen, bear this swag device. On the domed cover it will be seen, repeated in two scales.

Again, one sees throughout the service the repetitive use of medium plain diamonds: they occur as single bands encircling the vessels and also in broad fields or areas as on the domed cover. The meticulously executed fine fluting, on the urn, on the 'tub' and the dome cover, is still another characteristic cutting device repeatedly observed on single pieces in our study (cf. Plate 26A, showing a muffineer with Irish hallmarked silver cap; Plate 58, swag cut ewer).

It would be burdensome at this stage to list still further similarities between this Waterford service and the other examples of Waterford glass illustrated in our Plates and discussed in the text. The Waterford style is wonderfully summarized in this service and we could indeed wish that a Cork or a Dublin or a Belfast style were as explicitly stated.

### (c) The Duke of Wellington's Service[2]

As one studies the magnificent glass service of the Duke of Wellington, one realizes that the Age of Exuberance in Irish glass is here in full flower. The international style of the 1800's is close at hand, but characteristics throughout the service are sufficient, notwithstanding the international style, to relate the service to Ireland.

Specifically, reference is made to the pillar flutes enclosing fields of fine diamonds (Plate 92A); to decanters (Plate 91B) which in profile, neck and lip treatment are reminiscent of the Cork Municipal School of Art ewers and decanters in Plate 55C; to a ewer (Plate 92C) which also

---

[1] In a letter of March 14, 1931, attesting his belief in the Waterford origin of this service, M. S. Dudley Westropp referred to these eared bowls as 'tubs'. (A copy of the letter, dating the service 'about 1820', is displayed in the glass cabinet in the City Hall.) They are also referred to as ice pails, probably meaning bowls in which chilled (iced) desserts were served. It is most unlikely that ice – as in a present contemporary sense – would have been used in such vessels.

[2] Reference to the Duke of Wellington is always to the first Duke of Wellington unless otherwise noted.

reflects the same, repeating prismatic cutting, swan neck handle and an interesting vertical prismatic detail at the base of the handle.

Most important evidence of Irish provenance is the bowl with turned-over rim, on its stand (Plate 91A), one of a pair. This type of Irish bowl was described in Chapter 8a (Plates 43A, 43B), and the curious bowl stand was noticed in Chapter 8c (Plate 85c*b*). The prismatic work on the stand and its rim of flutes in vertical edging should not be overlooked.

Throughout this Wellington service there is a lavish use of strawberry diamonds, 'the favorite . . . motive . . . in the late (1830) Waterford designs'.[1]

Prismatic cutting and strawberry diamonds are insufficient grounds on which to affirm a definite Waterford origin for the Wellington service, although it may well date to about 1830 and thus fits comfortably the quotation from Thorpe above. It was the prestige factory of course, with its fame firmly built upon the standards of the Hill-Gatchell period terminating in 1799, but other factories were also at work in 1820–1830 as a glance at the table heading Chapter 4 will show. Formidable in the competitive picture are the two Cork houses (Waterloo and Terrace), both of which began operations after the Union of 1800; and in this connexion the composite style of Waterloo's marked decanters will be borne in mind. In Dublin the Williams family, notable for having started operations as early as 1764, survived the Union until 1827, while Mulvaney's uneven career did not close until 1835.

The practice of cutting glass elsewhere than where it was made may be emphasized here. Undermining any wishful thinking or false confidence which may exist where Waterford attribution is concerned, is an advertisement in the *Belfast News-Letter* as late as October 31, 1815, inserted by Jane Cleland, to the effect that 'she has imported from Waterford a quantity of plain flint glass, which she has got cut to the newest and richest patterns'.[2]

While, therefore, the evidence points to an Irish origin for the service, so many Irish hallmarks being present, a more specific attribution to Waterford or another centre must remain undetermined.

The service has notable details to which attention may be drawn because they are so unusual. The bowl in Plate 92A is heart-shaped. The

[1] Thorpe, p. 254.
[2] Westropp, p. 200. Also, Cleland is a recurring name in the Down Hunt account book records. One entry for 1791 is for 'Cleland the Glass Man's Bill'; another for 1798 is 'Jas. Cleland for three dozen wine glasses'; further entries occur through 1820. See also note 1, page 95, for another reference to the Down Hunt account book records.

circular leaf dishes are fan-cut beneath, each fan spine being covered (where width permits) with strawberry diamonds. There are two sizes of decanters; all stoppers are matched.[1] In addition to pieces shown in the plates, there are in the service three sizes of oval bowls, ranging in length from a bowl 11¾in. long, undoubtedly for serving, to small dishes for individual place-settings; there are carafes for water, conforming to the decanters in profile and cutting but without stoppers and not ground to receive stoppers; there are sugar bowls and finger bowls with two lips, all with flutes in vertical edging and rayed beneath; and there is a most unusual long, deep dish, the end walls of which are concave and cut with vertical prismatic motifs while the side walls are gently convex and wholly covered with strawberry diamonds (reminiscent of the cucumber dish, Plate 65B).

The service, as it survives after at least 125 years, remains so large that it can be divided between the present Duke of Wellington's two residences. The part of the service from which the illustrations were taken consists of approximately sixty pieces divided between thirteen different sizes and types of vessel.

There are no records to reveal from where or when the Duke of Wellington acquired this service. But there are sound reasons to support the suggested Irish provenance and the approximate 1830 date, quite apart from reasons of style and the calibre of the glass.

The Duke was born in Dublin in 1769. His father was Garrett Wellesley (or Wesley), first Earl of Mornington, and his mother the daughter of Vicount Dungannon.[2] Although his boyhood was spent in England and on the Continent, he returned to Ireland as aide-de-camp to two Lords Lieutenant of Ireland, beginning at the age of 18, and subsequently he represented in Parliament the Irish constituency of Trim, from 1790 to 1795.[3] Thus the future Duke had deep roots in Ireland and especially in the capital city.

Later in the Duke's life there were two occasions on which it was possible he might have obtained the glass service. The first was after the Battle of Waterloo, when he was the recipient of not only great honours but also magnificent gifts. During this period the Parliamentary Commissioners bought for him the estate of Stratfield Saye, and he himself acquired Apsley House at Hyde Park Corner (the present Wellington Museum). It is possible that the service was one of the

[1] The decanters are shown in a silver gilt waggon the origin of which is the subject of our Appendix F.

[2] In connexion with the latter name, the Williamite decanter engraved 'Loyal Dungannon', Plates 49B, 49C will be recalled.

[3] Trim is in Co. Meath, and only a short distance northwest of Dublin.

magnificent gifts with which the Duke was honoured, or that, with two residences to be equipped, the Duke himself ordered the service for one or another of them. If acquired at this time, the date of the service would be somewhat earlier than the approximate 1830 date suggested for it.

While the service does not have the appearance of Cork work as we know it, our knowledge of *later* Cork work is meagre and it should not be overlooked that the glass house of *Waterloo Co. Cork* was founded in the same year as the Waterloo victory.

The second occasion on which the Duke might have acquired the glass service occurred *c.* 1828–1829–1830. In the first of those years the Duke undertook alterations to Apsley House, a work resulting in the creation of the Waterloo Gallery, scene from 1830 to 1852 of the annual Waterloo Banquet.

This commemorative dinner had begun as an annual reunion, held on Waterloo Day, June 18. Initially it was attended by about 20 of the Duke's generals and held in the Apsley House dining room. With the completion of the 90 foot long Waterloo Gallery, the guest list was greatly increased; officers who had held junior rank in 1815 were now included; and as shown in the William Salter painting of the occasion, in 1836 the dinner was honoured by the presence of both King William IV and King William I of Holland.

In support of the theory that the Wellington service was acquired about 1830 because of the increased scale of the Waterloo dinners are two facts: apparently no other service has survived in quantity suitable to have been used for such splendid functions, and the service stylistically dates from about that time. . . . Admittedly one is indulging here in speculation, but until some firm facts come to light, speculation is the only course open and must be treated with the same caution as family tradition.

### (d) The Marquess of Bute's Service

The present chapter on Services is closed with four pieces (Plates 93A, 93Ba, b, 93C) from what was obviously a considerable service (cf. p. 141).[1]

The Irish features which they have in common, in addition to superb quality, will be recognized: wide fields of plain sharp diamonds and heavy pillar flutes. Individual Irish features are, of course, the button

[1] The famed Irish glass collection formed by the fourth Marquess of Bute (1881–1947) is supported by archives which provide an invaluable record of the state of Irish glass early in the twentieth century when the collection was begun. These matters are discussed in Appendix G.

finial on the melon-shaped bowl, and, on the jug, the small spout, the scalloped rim, the applied handle which has been both cut and shaped at its lower end. It will be of interest to compare this jug of the Bute Service with the examples in Plates 59A, 59B, 60A and 60B. The capacity of pillar flutes to reflect light is clearly shown on the melon bowl and on the jug in question.

It is clear that the boss of the bowl in Plate 93C, which is covered with chequered diamonds, is intended to fit into a stand as in Plate 43A. The illustration does justice to the crispness with which the fan scalloped edge has been cut.

The Samuel Miller patterns very clearly show the use of pillar flutes, diamond fields and fan cut rims on the bodies of bowls and sugars produced by the Waterford factory. On the strength of the patterns, the Marquess of Bute examples may with some confidence be attributed to Waterford and given an approximate date of 1820–1830[1].

[1] Although its English origin precludes illustration of it in this book, comment on glass services must include mention of the service of over 200 pieces belonging to the Marquess of Londonderry. It was made in 1824 by the Wear Flint Glass Co. of Sunderland; it is elaborately cut in the international style and engraved with the arms of Charles, third Marquess of Londonderry (1778–1854).

# Appendix A

## Glossary of Irish Cutting Terms Most Frequently Used in the Text, Keyed to the Illustrations

BLAZES close parallel incisions rising from a common horizontal line; they may be uniform or of unequal height; they include:
>    perpendicular blazes, 68D
>    slanting blazes, 41C, 68D
>    herringbone blazes

DIAMONDS in numerous variations of shape and depth; they include:
>    fine (or tiny) diamonds, as in a Waterford pillar and arch, 10B; pendent swag, 38C; panel, 83A.
>
>    plain diamonds, generally sharp and medium size but may be graduated; occur as bands, 41B; or as wide fields, 54B.
>
>    shallow diamonds, may be square and small (from $\frac{1}{2}$in.) to large (1in.), or oblong; in either case, cut flat with minimum projection; occur as standing rims in single bands, 69C, 61A, or double bands; occur as two or more bands, 32A, or as fields, 30A.
>
>    lozenge diamonds; a diamond, within a circular or oval depression, containing one or two smaller diamonds, the inner-most often being small shallow diamond(s) or medium plain diamonds; cut flat with minimum projection, 54Aa.
>
>    strawberry diamonds; plateau, generally square, formed by intersecting prismatic cuts; the flat plateau surface is cut with fine diamonds; used as a field, 79B; in lower relief, may be used as a single row, 13B, or isolated motif, 18A.
>
>    crosscut diamond; plateau as above, surface cut with single small star, also called 'hobnail cutting', 79D.

FACET CUTTING used for finials, 28B, knops, 72Ab; handles, 58B.

FACETS generally called 'large hollow facets'; uniform depressions of roughly oval shape, nested in two or more bands; generally used in the round, 41C, 54Aa.

FLUTES term freely used; flutes range from flat surface cutting of large areas, 62B, to cutting of narrow, deeply incised grooves.

    flat flutes; short and wide, 73A; tapered, 26A, 56.

    comb flutes, vertical cuts encircling a vessel, 38A; or in groups, 51A.

    pillar flutes, half round columns, also called lustre cutting; may be very short, 84C*a*, or long, 55B; may be tapered.

    flutes rayed beneath, as alternate for star cut beneath, 77D.

    flutes enclosed in vesica, 63B; vary in scale, may be fine, 80B*a*, or bold, 63B.

    flutes enclosed in band, 59A, 77D.

    flutes in vertical edging: $\frac{1}{4}$in. to 1in. in height, occur on standing rims, 34C, 68E, or on rims of covers and bodies of urns, jars, as 33, 68D.

FOOT circular, 69B; square, 30A; petalled, 58; domed, 41C; folded (the edge turned under, providing double thickness), moulded, 81C; stepped, 30A; with serrated edge, 79B.

GEOMETRIC CUTTING continuous chevron design, rendered very flat, usually providing a step between flat areas, 61B, 62A, 83C.

HUSK MOTIF occurs in bands, 28B, 86C, or in a swag (festoon), 7A; also referred to as 'arrowheads'.

PRINTIES depressions which may be circular, 57, or oval, 34B.

PRISMATIC CUTTING graphically mis-called 'step cutting'; V grooves parallel and generally contiguous, generally used in the round, 50A; may occur in panels, 65B; or on undersides of flat articles, 77B; single or double prismatic cuts divide the length of long flat flutes, 8B; very heavy prismatic cutting occurs on necks of jugs, 54B, and on candlesticks, 34B.

PRISMS refracting ornaments hung on fixtures, 36; not to be confused with –

PRISMS generally called 'alternate prisms'; contiguous parallel bands, cut to produce alternating grooves and ridges; most frequently found on turned-over rims of bowls, 41C.

RIMS top surface of rim may be lightly serrated, 57; with medium serrations, 60B; or if deeply serrated on a very thick wall of a vessel, 79B, serrations become flutes; also –

    fan scalloped, 43B,

    rounded scalloped, 55A, 78D,

    pointed scalloped, 27A*d*,

    trefoil (Van Dyke), 40A, 40B

SPLITS two short cuts form a V with vertical cut bisecting the angle; generally used above and below point of contact of two vesicas or two swags, 12, 18A.

STARS cut upon bottoms of decanters, jugs, etc., vary widely in number of points, rendering, etc.; indicate a late date; stars also occur enclosed in vesicas, 51B, 63B, or within –

STEPPED AREAS, CIRCULAR OR OVAL CUT VERY FLAT these may enclose stars, 78A*b*, or be the platform (as on the top of a cover of a jar) carrying the shank of the finial, 68D, 9B.

SWAG half circle or half oval area, usually pendent, filled with fine diamonds, 41E, or fine flutes, 58; or –

SWAG single, double, or more uniformly looped incisions, 58.

VESICA oval motif created by curved, flat cut incisions, 6B, 42B, 51B; generally elongated; a motif more frequently used in engraving than in cutting.

# Appendix B
## A Note Concerning
## Vessels with Notched Rims

There are three distinct types of vessel with one or two notches or lips on their rims. In this study they have been referred to as finger bowls (Plate 14A), as tumblers (Plates 72B*b* and 73A), and as mixing glasses (Plate 75D).

The vessel called a finger bowl has been variously used or thought to have been used for: (1), rinsing the mouth after eating; (2), rinsing the fingers after eating; (3), cooling wine glasses in chilled water at the table; (4), rinsing wine glasses at the table. It has been called a finger basin, a water glass and a wine cooler.

It is entirely possible that the bowl in question served all the purposes mentioned, with the period of one use overlapping the period of another. Also, one stratum of society might have adopted a secondary use earlier than another, or the changes may have been adopted in one locale sooner than in another.

An early reference which indicates the mouth rinsing use comes from Tobias Smollet who expressed disgust in 1766 over the 'beastly' custom observed in his travels of using water glasses for the purpose. Another reference, cited by Thorpe,[1] indicates that a few years after Smollett a second traveller was likewise disgusted by the 'filthy custom of using water-glasses after meals (which) is as common (sc. in Ireland) as in England . . .'.[2] In 1784 la Rochefoucauld found the custom 'extremely unfortunate' (Appendix C).

The use of the finger bowl *as* a finger bowl is also mentioned by la Rochefoucauld. Possibly vessels with rims not having lips were reserved for that purpose. A late eighteenth-century example is shown in Plate 20B, the bowl marked *Francis Collins Dublin* and engraved with the crowned harp and the 'Royal Dublin Infantry' inscription.

A contemporary reference which suggests the use of the finger bowl as a monteith is the bill of sale (Chapter 9, footnote 2) rendered to the Prince of Wales in 1807. A list of glasses of numerous types is headed by

[1] Thorpe, p. 332.     [2] ibid.

'48 montieths' [*sic*], but whether the monteiths were used for glass cooling or glass rinsing is not known.

Although the practice is known to have been followed, it is hard to believe that *cooling* wine glasses at the table was general, because it implies a dearth of glasses which seems improbable. The theory of using the notched bowls for *rinsing* glasses at the table, and especially glasses used for port, is supported by several of la Rochefoucauld's comments. These have to do with the withdrawal of the servants from the dining room after the dinner, and the quality of the port which was consumed in quantity. La Rochefoucauld found it 'bad and thick'. Port is notable for the sediment it throws, which it would be desirable to remove from the glass before refilling it.

It seems improbable that tumbler-scaled vessels with single notch lips were used as finger bowls but they might have served for rinsing purposes, or more likely, as individual mixing glasses. In their stemmed version they are sometimes found today in broken sets of two or three. The *Cork Corporation* glass (Plate 75D) was very probably a mixing glass because of its 7in. height and ample capacity.

# Appendix C

## Excerpt from
## *A Frenchman in England, 1784*

FRANCOIS DE LA ROCHEFOUCAULD
translated with notes by S. C. Roberts,
Cambridge University Press, 1933

---

The following describes the dinner and social evening customs of the Anglo-Irish Revival period, with particular reference to the quantity of glass required in a well-appointed house.

After commenting on dinner, 'one of the most wearisome of English experiences,' which he says lasts 'for four or five hours', la Rochefoucauld continues:

'After the sweets, you are given water in small bowls of very clean glass in order to rinse out your mouth – a custom which strikes me as extremely unfortunate. The more fashionable folk do not rinse out their mouths, but that seems to me even worse; for, if you use the water to wash your hands, it becomes dirty and quite disgusting. The ceremony over, the cloth is removed . . . the table is covered with all kinds of wine, for even gentlemen of modest means always keep a large stock of good wine. On the middle of the table is a small quantity of fruit, a few biscuits (to stimulate thirst) and some butter, for many English people take it at dessert.

'At this point all the servants disappear. The ladies drink a glass or two of wine and at the end of a half an hour all go out together. It is then that real enjoyment begins – there is not an Englishman who is not supremely happy at this particular moment. One proceeds to drink – sometimes in an alarming measure. Everyone has to drink in his turn, for the bottle makes a continuous circuit of the table and the host takes note that everyone is drinking in his turn. After this has gone on for some time and mere thirst has become an inadequate reason for drinking, a fresh stimulus is supplied by the drinking of "toasts", that is to say, the host begins by giving the name of a lady; he drinks to her health and everyone is obliged to do likewise. After the host someone else gives a toast and everyone drinks to the health of everyone else's lady. Then each member of the party names some man and the whole ceremony begins again. ... The sideboard too is furnished with a number of chamber pots and it is a common practice to relieve oneself while the rest are drinking; one has no kind of concealment and the practice strikes me as most indecent.

'At the end of two or three hours a servant announces that tea is ready and conducts the gentlemen from their drinking to join the ladies in the drawing room, where they are usually employed in making tea or coffee. After making tea, one generally plays whist, and at midnight there is cold meat for those who are hungry. While the game is going on, there is punch on a table for those who want it.'

# Appendix D

*Receipts for Makeing Flint Enamel, blue & Best Green Glass, always used by John Hill – 17th May 1786 –*

Flint ——
4. 1. 9 Sand..
3 – 0. 10 Lead –
1. 1. 0 Ashes –
14. Salt Petre
6 oz Magnesse

you will see by the proof Taken in Melting. if to high Cloured use a little Arsenick. if to low add more Mag: nere —

Enamel ——
2.. 2. 20 Sand
3 – 0. 24 Lead
3.. 14 Salt Petre
24 Arsenick

put but a Small Melting in the pot for the first time, and so on Every Melting for if you put to Much at a time it will boil over ————

you may use Enamel Cullet if you have it with the batch —

For Blue ——

Use the flint batch & any Sort of Cullet & about 8 oz of Saphora to Every 20 of Cullet or batch, but Saphora differs so much in Quality, that there is no Certain Rule for Quantity – but Judge of the Colour by the proofs in Melting

For Green ——

Use flint batch & Cullet & to Every 20 put 8 oz Calcined Copper pounded fine – if not Dark enough use more Copper –

'Receipts for Making Flint, Enamel, blue & Best Green Glass, always used by John Hill – 17th May 1786.' The formulae dictated by John Hill to Jonathan Gatchell. Gatchell Letters, Waterford Glassworks, No. 1–78, 154–1956, Vol. 1; document 7(d). By courtesy of the National Museum of Ireland. (See Chapter 3c)

# Appendix E

# A Note on 'Waterford' Chandeliers and Other Lighting Fixtures

Excluded from this study has been consideration of the so-called 'Waterford' chandelier or related lighting devices such as portable table fixtures or sconces, customarily dripping with faceted diamonds, prisms or other reflection drops. The reason for this is that with the exception of a chandelier in a London museum,[1] which has a history (unverified) of coming from Thomastown, Co. Killkenny, near Waterford, the writer has not located any lighting fixture with a positive Irish provenance. Curious as it may seem, the fact is that no indisputably Irish example of the chandelier, the object most frequently termed 'Waterford', has made its appearance.

The Assembly Rooms's chandeliers at Bath, long associated with Waterford in the popular mind, have been conclusively proved to be of London origin and to have been made before the Waterford Glass House was opened.[2]

Again, the attribution to Waterford of the chandelier in Independence Hall, Philadelphia, cannot be confirmed because 'the only sure thing about the chandelier is that it hung in Independence Hall from 1846 to 1955'.[3] From a list in the writer's possession of restoration work performed in 1923–1924 on the Independence Hall chandelier, it is fair to say that even if the chandelier were initially of Waterford origin, very little of it is of Waterford origin today.

Citing another well-known American example: there is no documentation of Waterford origin for the matching set of chandeliers in St. Paul's Chapel, Trinity Parish, New York.[4]

The chandelier hanging in Waterford's City Hall Council Chamber gives little evidence of how a truly Waterford Glass House chandelier might have appeared. Even Westropp, a born Irishman with a wealth of

[1] Victoria and Albert Museum, Ac. No. C.5–1931, Given by Major W. H. Mulville.
[2] *The Connoisseur*, October, 1938, pp. 187 *et seqq.*, article: 'The Eighteenth Century Chandeliers at Bath', by J. Bernard Perret.
[3] Correspondence, Author's files.
[4] ibid.

local connexions and entrée into local archives, was unable to obtain documentary evidence of the alleged fact that the Council Chamber chandelier was given to the city of Waterford by the Glass House.[1]

Our best information on the subject of chandeliers is perhaps in the concluding paragraph of Mr. Perret's article already cited. Writing of the Thomastown example, he says if it be true that the Thomastown chandelier was made in Waterford, 'it establishes that Irish factories copied the designs which were popular in London twenty years previously.' While an 'Irish style' has manifested itself in table and other glass ware, it cannot be shown to have done so where lighting fixtures are concerned.

[1] Westropp, p. 190.

# Appendix F

# Excerpt from Sir Edward Thomason's Memoirs, Vol. II

Longman, Brown, Green, and Longmans, London, 1845

---

The following pertains to the pair of silver gilt decanter waggons, in the collection of the present, the 7th, Duke of Wellington, K.G., one of which is shown in Plate 91B.

'Now the facts are as follows: – Many years since, Lord Rolle called upon me at my establishment, and said that he had dined with his Majesty, George IV, the day before, and that his Majesty was pleased to remark that he regretted that his noble guests who sat on either side of him were constrained to rise from their seats to pass the wine; and observed to him (Lord Rolle), as you have said that you are going to Birmingham tomorrow, you had better call upon Thomason, who may invent some plan to obviate this inconvenience.

'I suggested to Lord Rolle that decanter stands upon wheels was, in my opinion, the only method to be adopted; and as I held the beautiful dies containing the victories of the late war, forty in number, viz., from the landing in Portugal to the capture of Paris, and the settling of Napoleon at St. Helena, I recommended to place these medals around the flat perpendicular edges of the bottle stands, which would fill up four, thereby adapting them to two waggons, the whole made of silver and richly gilt, and each waggon to have four beautifully ornamented wheels. His lordship approved of my suggestions, and requested that no time should be lost in executing them; and, when done, to forward them to the Marquis of Conyingham. On their arrival, his Majesty expressed his entire approbation of the thought. Sometime afterwards the King presented them to the Duke of Wellington.'

It will be readily understood that the gentlemen seated at the banquet table on either side of the Sovereign might not shove the decanter from one to another, in front of him, nor would it have been suitable for the King to assist in the passing of the decanters from one side to another.

Hence Sir Edward's solution of a waggon, which measures 13in. in length without handle, the rolling of which in front of the Sovereign was considered more suitable than pushing a decanter slide.

The medal immediately to the right of the rear wheel depicts 'England Gives Peace to the World'; the two medals immediately to the right of the front wheel commemorate 'Salamanca July XXII, MDCCCXII' and 'British Army Enters Madrid Aug XII MDCCCXII'.

# Appendix G

## An Historical Note on The Marquess of Bute's Collection

The story of Irish glass of the Age of Exuberance is enriched by archives belonging to the Marquess of Bute. In a wealth of correspondence these archives describe the state of Irish glass early in the twentieth century, particularly in Dublin. They show with engrossing detail how a great collection was assembled in that time when Irish glass of the period of from 1780 to 1835 had barely acquired the age or reputation of the antique.

The fourth Marquess began to acquire Irish glass about the year 1911. While his early purchases were made in London, in the year 1915 the name of M. S. Dudley Westropp in Dublin begins to crop up in the archives, and from 1915 forward for a decade or more Westropp advised the Marquess on his collecting interests.

Westropp was a native of Cork. At the beginning of the century, after ten years Army service concluding with a year (1897–1898) in South Africa with the Irish Rifles, he had begun an association with the National Museum which was to last until his retirement in 1936. By 1915 he was in a unique position to counsel because of his training, his professional status, and his residence in Dublin.[1]

In his capacity as a museum curator, Westropp was continually approached by both private individuals and dealers who had treasures of glass to sell. When the Museum was not interested, the fourth Marquess' collection might be enriched by professionally vetted acquisitions of prime quality and, today, of the greatest rarity.

The Museum frequently was not interested in articles which came upon the market, perhaps because they were duplicates of examples the Museum already had, or the moment was not propitious for Museum buying. In one of his letters Westropp wrote: 'there is not much use in trying (to interest the Museum in a certain piece) under present circumstances'; and again: 'the only reason I did not take them in the Museum is that we had not room.'

As time went on the fourth Marquess became known in Ireland as a

[1] See bibliography: *Glass-Making in Ireland* was published in 1911; *Irish Glass* was published in 1920.

146

collector of Irish antiquities, and was consequently approached directly by individuals with heirlooms to sell. During part of this collecting period his Librarian was W. J. Stanley, an Irishman not unknown to Dublin dealers. Much of the correspondence which led to Westropp's influence upon the Marquess' collection was carried on through Stanley. Frequently Westropp would report about articles he thought would interest the Marquess; and in turn, Stanley, on behalf of Lord Bute, would ask Westropp's opinion as a qualified and on-the-scene advisor, about an article which the Marquess had been offered directly.

The relationship was sufficiently amiable for Westropp, on occasion, to store at the Museum purchases made by the Marquess pending their shipment to Scotland, and on other occasions, the Museum was the gainer when Westropp would put on Museum exhibition an article loaned by Lord Bute for display before it was shipped to him.

Nowhere are the Bute archives more arresting than in the light they throw on what was available and what was thought to be choice at the time. Thus in April, 1918, Westropp wrote to Stanley: 'Does he (Lord Bute) want any good glass bowls as good ones are turning up over here. . . . Of course circular ones do not bring near as much as boat shaped ones.' (Sketches, end of Appendix.)

Late in the same year the order of the correspondence is reversed: Stanley wrote to Westropp: 'I have just had a letter from His Lordship in which he states that he is beginning to be somewhat sceptical about the large glass bowl which he purchased . . . now on view in the Museum. There is such a lot of glass being faked nowadays. He wishes me to write and ask you if there is any history attached to this bowl; and he adds about yourself: "I know he is as knowledgeable on such affairs as anyone, but all admit the difficulties of glass." ' To this scepticism about the genuineness of the bowl, Westropp replied, indicating his familiarity with local Irish sources: 'It (the bowl) belonged to a Miss Somerville . . . she lent it to the Museum . . . it had been in her family a long time. . . . I do not have any doubts whatsoever about the genuineness of the bowl, so I do not think Lord Bute may be at all anxious about its being a fake.'

In June, 1919, Westropp told Stanley that he had stowed into the Museum safe a glass urn (Sketch, end of Appendix), which the Marquess had bought. It stood on a high domed base and was cut with two ranges of long, flat tapered flutes. It was truly a prime piece for a collector and on the margin of the sketch Lord Bute wrote unequivocally: 'Yes – will take this glass.' His acumen has been proven by time, for the piece is of the utmost rarity today.

On another occasion, in July, 1925, Westropp furnished a sketch

(Sketch, end of Appendix) about which he wrote to Stanley: 'I saw a very fine piece of glass here the other day & thought perhaps Lord Bute would be interested in it. It is an Irish piece I should say probably Dublin or Cork of about 1800 or perhaps a little earlier – a very fine candle lamp[1] which could be, of course, adapted to electric light. . . . I have never seen such a large one of these . . . I would recommend it for the Museum as we have nothing like it' but 'present circumstances' constrained him from doing so.

Throughout the correspondence, the terms candle lamp, candle light and glass pendant are used synonymously.

In November, 1926, a flurry of correspondence began regarding a choice pair of Williamite decanters and four matching cordial glasses. Initially Westropp recommended them, and then a Dublin dealer wrote following up. These pieces are almost certainly the ones which today belong to the Philadelphia Museum of Art, Bequest of George H. Lorimer, judging by Westropp's description of them and a drawing he submitted. 'There are two decanters,' he wrote, '(a pair) engraved with a bust of King William, a large harp and crown and badge (?) of flags trophies etc on the other side. Also 4 wine glasses on tall stems, the bowls engraved in a similar way as the decanters with bust of King William and harp crowned. They are probably Irish glass about 1750 or a little earlier. They are a most exceptional lot. The two decanters are probably unique. I have never heard or seen of a similar pair. Something this shape (sketch). They are complete with pointed stoppers.' In December, 1926, Westropp wrote about them again, fearing his first letter had been lost; in January and April, 1927, there is still more correspondence, but apparently Lord Bute did not follow Westropp's recommendation in this instance.[2]

Today's piece-by-piece collector must view with envy the opportunity given to Lord Bute to acquire *at one time* a collection of Irish glass numbering nearly eighty pieces. Although it was largely on exhibit at the Museum, it was offered directly to the Marquess by its owner. At Stanley's request, Westropp passed judgement upon it. It does not appear that Lord Bute bought the entire lot, but certain pieces, listed and sketched by Westropp, are presently in the Marquess of Bute collection. These include a ship's decanter, a handled ewer with pronounced spout,[3] pickle jars (Plate 69D *a, b, c*), etc.

[1] cf. Plate 86c.

[2] These same glasses were described by Hartshorne in 1897. At that time they were 24 in number. When the pair of decanters and four wine glasses described by Westropp reached Philadelphia, the four wines had increased in number to 12.

[3] cf. Plates 54B, 54C.

The collection also includes a bowl and stand virtually identical to the example illustrated in Plates 43B, 43A, attributed to Waterford. There is also a *Penrose Waterford* impressed decanter with cut swags filled with fine diamonds similar to the one illustrated in Plate 12, which was also an impressed *Penrose Waterford* piece.

Unfortunately, the archives have not yet yielded information regarding the service of which we show four examples (Plates 96C, 96B, 96A *a, b*).

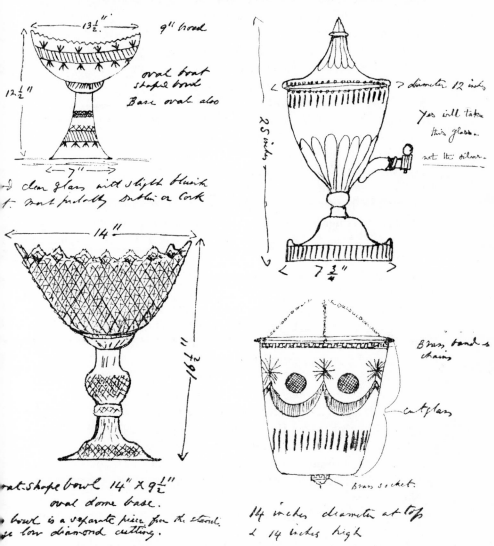

Four sketches of Irish glass available in Dublin in the early twentieth century and submitted to the Marquess of Bute by M. S. Dudley Westropp. Bowls, urn and candle lamp are all referred to in the Bute-Westropp correspondence.

# Bibliography

GLASS REFERENCES

Buckley, Francis, *A History of Old English Glass*, London, 1925

Buckley, W., *European Glass*, London, 1926

Chambon, Raymond, 'La Verrerie des XIX et XX Siècles' in *Trois Millénaires d'Art Verrier*, Musée Curtius, Liège, 1958

Charleston, Robert J., 'Waterford Glass', *Antiques*, June 1956

Daniel, Dorothy, *Cut and Engraved Glass 1771–1905*, New York, 1950

Davis, Derek C., *English and Irish Antique Glass*, London, 1964

[Harding Walter], *Old Irish Glass: the 'Walter Harding' Collection Including Old English and Other Pieces*, author not named (Mrs. Graydon Stannus?), 1930

Hartshorne, A., *Old English Glasses*, London, 1897

Haynes, E. Barrington, *Glass Through the Ages*, revised edition, Harmondsworth, 1959

Haynes, E. Barrington, 'Glass from Ireland', *Antiques*, March 1950

Hughes, G. Bernard, *English, Scottish and Irish Table Glass*, London, 1956

Hughes, J. J., foreword in catalogue, *Exhibition of Waterford Glass*, Waterford, 1952

Hutton, William, *European Glass*, Toledo Museum of Art, undated

MacLeod, Catriona, 'Late Eighteenth Century Dublin Finger Bowls in the National Museum of Ireland', *Journal of the Royal Society of Antiquaries of Ireland* vol. 96, part 2, 1966

MacLeod, Catriona, 'Irish Volunteer Glass', *Journal of the Military History Society of Ireland*, vol. VII, no. 28, summer 1966

MacMullen, H. T., 'Waterford Glass I', *Country Life*, August 30, 1946; 'Waterford Glass II', *Country Life*, September 6, 1946

McKearin, Geo. P. and Helen, *American Glass*, New York, 1946

Pellatt, Apsley, *Curiosities of Glass Making* . . . London, 1849

Seaby, W. S., *Irish Williamite Glass*, Ulster Museum, Belfast, publication No. 174, 1965

Stannus, Mrs. Graydon, *Old Irish Glass*, The Connoisseur, London, 1920

Thorpe, W. A., *A History of English and Irish Glass*, Medici Society, London, 1929

Wakefield, Hugh, *Nineteenth Century British Glass*, London, 1961

# Bibliography

Westropp, M. S. Dudley, R.I.A., *Irish Glass: An Account of Glass-Making in Ireland from the XVIth Century to the Present Day*, London, undated (1920)

Westropp, M. S. Dudley, R.I.A., 'Glass-Making in Ireland', *Proceedings of the Royal Irish Academy*, vol. XXIX, section C, no. 3, Dublin, 1911

Westropp, M.S. Dudley, R.I.A., 'Moulded Glass', *Antiques*, December 1928

Winchester, Alice, editorial in *Antiques*, June 1956

# Picture Credits

Photographs are from museum sources with the exceptions which follow for which acknowledgements are due: J. Banbury, Dublin: plates; 9A, 9B, 52A, 52C, 55C, 65A, 66B, 73A, 83A, 83B, 86B, 86C, 89A, 89B, 90A, 90B; Bassano Ltd., London: plates 40A, 75D; E. Irving Blomstrann, New Britain, Connecticut: plates 53A, 78B, 78E, 87A, 87B, 87C, 88A, 88B; J. Brendan Dalton, Waterford: plate 77E; Frank Dunand, New York: plates 33 43A; Raymond F. Errett, Corning, New York: plates 4C, 5B, 14A, 26A, 34A, 34B, 34C, 41D, 46A, 56, 60A, 61B, 63B, 65B, 68B, 73D, 75B, 77A, 77B, 77C, 78A, 79B, 79C, 79D, 80A, 80B, 85A, 85B, 85C, 86A; Wallace Heaton Ltd., London: plates 91A, 91B, 92A, 92B, 92C; F. Jewell-Harrison, Bedford: plates 8C, 10A, 66C; Ritter-Jeppesen Pty. Ltd., Melbourne: plates 28B, 49A, 62A, 71C, Studio Swain, Glasgow: plates; 41E, 62B, 65C, 69D, 75A, 77D, 93A, 93B, 93C and frontispiece; Richard Tarr, Exmouth (Devon): plates 47A, 52B, 74A, 82A, 82B; Taylor and Dull, New York: plates 16A, 16B, 29, 38C, 38D, 39A, 41B, 41C, 42B, 43B, 51A, 54A, 54B, 55A, 55B, 60A, 68C, 68D, 68E, 69C; colour plate C, courtesy Howard Phillips, London

# Index

# Index

chandeliers, 122, 142
colour of, 46
imitations of, 47
metal, 46
pattern drawings, 21
quality of, 46
receipts for, 41, 47, 141
Waterford Glass House, 38, 73, 124
Waterloo, Battle of, 49, 131
Banquet, 132
Waterloo Co. Cork, *see* Waterloo Glass
House Company
Glass House Company, 49, 75
Wellesley (Wesley), *see* Wellington,
Duke of
Wellington, Duke of, 129 ,131

Duke of, Collection, 94
Duke of, Service, 57, 129
Museum, 131
Westropp, family, 22, 112
M. S. Dudley, 41, 45, 46, 54, 106,
129, 146 *et seqq.*
R. M. L., Rev. 112
William III, 98, 110
Williams, Richard & Co., 33
Wright, John, 42
Jonathan, 41, 44, 45
Nathan, 42
Nehemiah, 42, 44
Samuel H., 41

'yacht jugs', 115

1. Decanter, marked *B. Edwards Belfast*. Ht. 11¼ in. with stopper. *c.* 1800. Ulster Museum, Belfast. (See page 68)

2A. Decanter, marked *B. Edwards Belfast*. Ht. 11 in. with stopper. *c.* 1800. The Corning Museum of Glass, Corning (New York). Ac. no. 50.2.30. (See pages 68, 69)

2B. Decanter, marked *B. Edwards Belfast*. Ht. 7½ in. *c.* 1800. By courtesy of the National Museum of Ireland. (See page 68)

3A. Decanter, marked *B. Edwards Belfast*. Ht. 6⅞ in. *c.* 1800. Ulster Museum, Belfast. (See pages 68, 69)

3B. Decanter, marked *B. Edwards Belfast*. Ht. 7 in. *c.* 1800. Ulster Museum, Belfast. (See pages 68, 69)

4A. Decanter, marked *B. Edwards Belfast*. Ht. 10¼ in. with stopper.
*c.* 1800. Ulster Museum, Belfast. (See pages 68, 69)

4B. Decanter, marked *B. Edwards Belfast*. Ht. 7¼ in. to lip. *c.* 1800.
By courtesy of the National Museum of Ireland. (See pages 68, 70)

4C. Pair of decanters, marked *B. Edwards Belfast*. Ht. 7 in. to lip. *c.* 1800.
Author's Collection. (See pages 69, 70, 73)

5A.
Decanter, marked *Cork Glass Co*. Ht. 8¾ in.
*c*. 1783–1818. By courtesy of the
National Museum of Ireland.
(See page 70)

5B.
Pair of decanters, marked
*Cork Glass Co*. Ht. 9⅝ in.
with grid stoppers.
*c*. 1783–1818.
Author's Collection.
(See pages 70, 71)

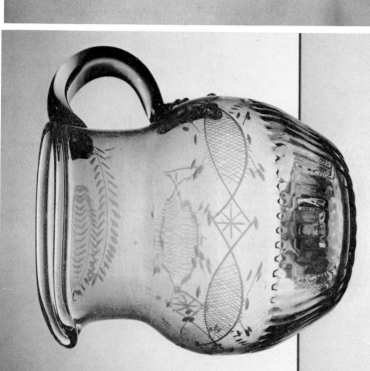

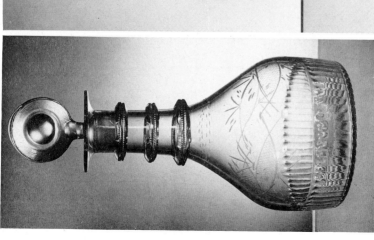

6A. Decanter, marked *Cork Glass Co.* Ht. 10½ in. with stopper. *c.* 1783–1818. The Corning Museum of Glass, Corning (New York). Ac. no. 50.2.32 (See pages 70, 71)

6B. Jug, marked *Cork Glass Co.* Ht. 6 in. *c.* 1783–1818. Courtesy of Victoria and Albert Museum. (See page 71)

6C. Decanter, marked *Cork Glass Co.* Ht. 10 in. with stopper. *c.* 1783–1818. The Corning Museum of Glass, Corning (New York). Ac. no. 55.2.2. (See pages 71, 76)

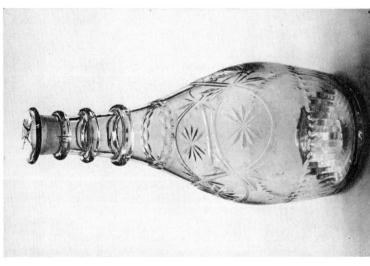

7A. Decanter, marked *Cork Glass Co.* Ht. 10⅞ in. with stopper. *c.* 1783–1818. Reproduced by permission of the Syndics of the Fitzwilliam Museum, Cambridge. (See pages 71–72)

7B. Decanter, marked *Cork Glass Co.* Ht. 9¼ in. *c.* 1783–1818. By courtesy of the National Museum of Ireland. (See page 72)

7C. Decanter, marked *Cork Glass Co.* Ht. 8 in. *c.* 1783–1818. By courtesy of the National Museum of Ireland. (See page 72)

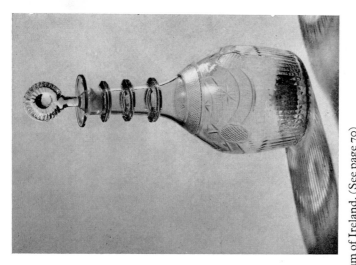

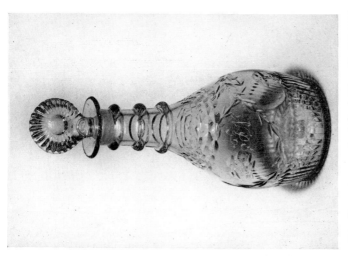

8A.  Decanter, marked *Cork Glass Co.* Ht. 8½ in. *c.* 1783–1818. By courtesy of the National Museum of Ireland. (See page 70)
8B.  Decanter, marked *Cork Glass Co.* Ht. 8¼ in. *c.* 1783–1818. By courtesy of the National Museum of Ireland. (See page 72)
8C.  Decanter, marked *Cork Glass Co.* Ht. 11 in. *c.* 1783–1818. By courtesy of the Cecil Higgins Art Gallery, Bedford. (See page 72)

9A. Dish, marked *Cork Glass Co.* Dia. 7⅛ in.; Ht. rim 1 in. *c.* 1783–1818.
Collection, Mr. Knollys Stokes, Cork. (See pages 72–73)

9B. Butter cooler, cover, with stand marked *Cork Glass Co.* Max. dia. 7⅛ in.
*c.* 1783–1818. Collection, Crawford Municipal School of Art, Cork,
Barrett Bequest. (See page 72)

10A. (*left, above*) Decanter, marked *Penrose Waterford*. Ht. 8½ in. with stopper. *c.* 1783–1799. By courtesy of the Cecil Higgins Art Gallery, Bedford. (See pages 73, 75)

10B. (*above*) Decanter, marked *Penrose Waterford*. Ht. 8½ in. to lip. *c.* 1783–1799. Courtesy of the Victoria and Albert Museum. (See pages 74, 77)

11. (*left*) Decanter, marked *Penrose Waterford*. Ht. 8 in. *c.* 1800. By courtesy of the National Museum of Ireland. (See pages 73, 75)

12. Decanter, marked *Penrose Waterford*. Ht. 8$\frac{3}{10}$ in. *c.* 1783–1799. By courtesy of the National Museum of Ireland. (See page 74)

13A.
Decanter, marked *Penrose
Waterford*. Ht. 8¼ in.
*c.* 1783–1799. By courtesy of the
National Museum of Ireland.
(See page 74)

13B.
Decanter, marked *Penrose
Waterford*. Ht. 9 in. *c.* 1783–1799.
Collection,
Reverend R. M. L. Westropp,
Windermere (Westmorland).
(See page 74)

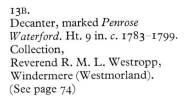

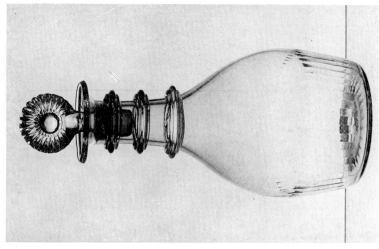

14A. Finger bowl, marked *Penrose Waterford*. Ht. $5\frac{3}{8}$ in.; dia. top, $4\frac{1}{8}$ in. *c.* 1783–1799. Author's Collection. (See pages 74–75, 137)
14B. Decanter, marked *Waterloo Co. Cork*. Ht. 9 in. with stopper. *c.* 1815–1820. The Toledo Museum of Art, Toledo (Ohio). (See page 75)

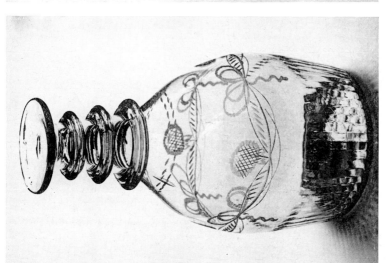

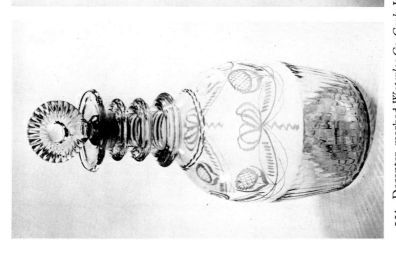

15A. Decanter, marked *Waterloo Co. Cork*. Ht. 10¼ in. with stopper. *c.* 1815–1820. Manchester City Art Galleries, Lloyd Roberts Bequest. (See pages 75–76)
15B. Decanter, marked *Waterloo Co. Cork*. Ht. 8 3/10 in. *c.* 1815–1820. By courtesy of the National Museum of Ireland. (See page 76)
15C. Decanter, marked *Waterloo Co. Cork*. Ht. 7 in. *c.* 1815–1820. By courtesy of the National Museum of Ireland. (See page 76)

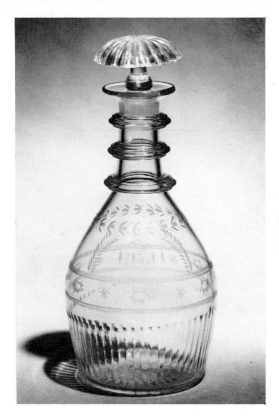

16A.
Decanter, marked *Waterloo Co. Cork*.
Ht. 8⅝ in. to lip. *c.* 1815–1820. Author's
Collection. (See page 76)

16B.
Bottom of decanter in Plate 16A showing
marked factory name. Author's Collection.
(See page 60, 76)

17A.
Jug, marked *Waterloo Co. Cork.*
Ht. 5⅞ in. *c.* 1815–1820. Courtesy
Victoria and Albert Museum.
(See page 76)

17B.
Jug, marked *Waterloo Co. Cork.*
Ht. 6⅝ in. *c.* 1815–1820.
The Toledo Museum of Art,
Toledo (Ohio). (See page 76)

18A.
Decanter, marked *Waterloo Co. Cork*.
Ht. 8 in. *c.* 1815–1820. By courtesy of the
National Museum of Ireland. (See page 77)

18B.
Decanter, marked *Waterloo Co. Cork*
Ht. 10¼ in. *c.* 1815–1820.
Reproduced by permission of the
Syndics of the Fitzwilliam Museum,
Cambridge. (See page 77)

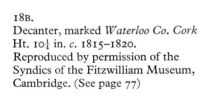

19A. Finger bowl, marked *Francis Collins Dublin*. Ht. 3⅕ in. *c.* 1800. By courtesy of the National Museum of Ireland. (See page 78)

19B. Butter cooler, marked *Francis Collins Dublin*, with cover. Ht. 5⅜ in. *c.* 1800. By courtesy of the National Museum of Ireland. (See page 78)

20A.
Decanter, marked *Francis Collins Dublin*. Ht. $8\frac{3}{10}$ in. *c.* 1800. By courtesy of the National Museum of Ireland. (See pages 72, 78)

20B.
Finger bowl, marked *Francis Collins Dublin*. Ht. $3\frac{2}{5}$ in. Late eighteenth century. By courtesy of the National Museum of Ireland. (See page 78)

21A. Finger bowl, marked *J. D. Ayckbowm Dublin.*
Ht. 3⅗ in. Late eighteenth – early nineteenth century.
By courtesy of the National Museum of Ireland.
(See page 79)

21B. Two dishes, moulded glass. (*a*) marked *J.D.A.* (*b*) marked *C.M. & Co.* Length, both,
approx. 10½ in. *c.* 1820. By courtesy of the National Museum of Ireland. (See page 79)

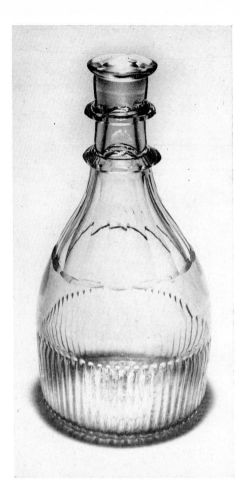

22. (*left, above*) Decanter, marked *Armstrong Ormond Quay* (Dublin). Ht. 8 in. *c.* 1800. By courtesy of the National Museum of Ireland. (See page 78)

23. (*left, below*) Finger bowl, marked *Mary Carter & Son 80 Grafton St Dublin*. Ht. $3\frac{3}{10}$ in. Late eighteenth – early nineteenth century. By courtesy of the National Museum of Ireland. (See page 79)

24. (*right, above*) Mug with coin in stem. Ht. $6\frac{7}{8}$ in. *c.* 1813. Manchester City Art Galleries, Lloyd Roberts Bequest. (See pages 22, 80)

25. (*right, below*) Bowl with coin in stem. Ht. $8\frac{1}{2}$ in. *c.* 1805. Collection of the Philadelphia Museum of Art, Bequest of George H. Lorimer. (See pages 22, 80)

26A.
Muffineer, silver top, Dublin, 1797. Ht. 7¾ in.
c. 1797. Author's Collection.
(See pages 22, 81)

26B.
Jar, silver top, Drogheda crest. Ht. 8½ in.
After 1781. Courtesy of the
Victoria and Albert Museum.
(See pages 22, 82)

27A. Five of 14 cut glass parts of centrepiece shown in Plate 27B.

27B. Centrepiece: silver frame with mark for Dublin, 1787. Frame length, 22½ in. *c.* 1787. Courtesy of the Victoria and Albert Museum. (See pages 22, 82–83)

28A.
Covered urn. Dia. cover rim, 5 in. *c.* 1790.
The Corning Museum of Glass, Corning
(New York). Ac. no. 51.2.244.
(See page 84)

28B.
Covered urn. Ht. 11 in. *c.* 1795.
Collection, Mrs. Neville Fraser,
Melbourne. (See pages 84–85)

29. Pair of covered urns. Ht. 12½ in. *c.* 1800. Author's Collection. (See page 85)

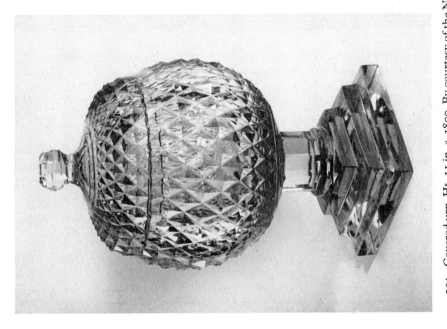

30A. Covered urn. Ht. 11 in. *c.* 1800. By courtesy of the National Museum of Ireland. (See page 85)
30B. Covered urn. Ht. (approx.) 9 in. *c.* 1820. Formerly on loan to the Victoria and Albert Museum from the Bles Collection. (See page 85)

31. Three matching covered urns. Ht. 7¾ in. *c.* 1815–1820. Courtesy of the Henry Ford Museum, Dearborn (Michigan). (See pages 85–86)

32. Pair of urns. Ht. 11 in. *c.* 1800–1815. The Corning Museum of Glass, Corning (New York). Ac. no. 51.2.190A, B. (See page 85)

33. Covered urn. Ht. 9½ in. *c.* 1820–1835. Author's Collection. (See pages 84, 86)

34A. Pair of moulded candlesticks. Ht. 6¼ in. *c.* 1780–1820.
Author's Collection. (See page 88)

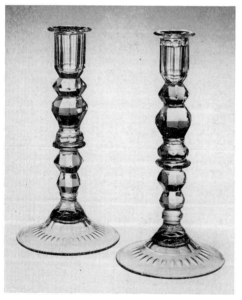

34B. Pair of candlesticks. Ht. 8⅞ in. *c.* 1790. Author's Collection. (See page 86)
34C. Pair of candlesticks. Ht. 5⅝ in. *c.* 1790. Author's Collection. (See page 87)

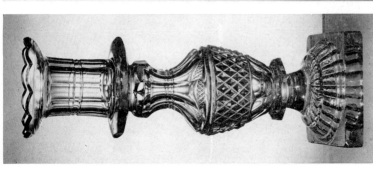

35A.  Candlestick. Ht. 8¼ in. *c.* 1800–1820. The Corning Museum of Glass, Corning (New York). Ac. no. 50.2.85B. (See page 87)
35B.  Pair of candlesticks. Ht. 5⅞ in. *c.* 1820. The Corning Museum of Glass, Corning (New York). Ac. no. 51.2.222A, B. (See page 87)

37A. Vase or commemorative drinking vessel. Ht. $11\frac{5}{8}$ in. Engraved: 1802.
Ulster Museum, Belfast (See pages 88–89)
37B. Vase, reverse of 37A.

36. (*facing page*) Candlestick. One of a pair. Hts. $9\frac{3}{4}$ in., 11 in. *c.* 1785.
The Corning Museum of Glass, Corning (New York). Ac. no. 50.2.21A.
(See pages 86–87)

38A. Vase or commemorative drinking vessel. Dated 1813. Ht. 11½ in. Courtesy of the Victoria and Albert Museum. (See page 89)

38B. Vase. Ht. 8¾ in. *c.* 1820–1830. By courtesy National Museum of Ireland. (See page 90)

38C. Vase. Ht. 7⅜ in. *c.* 1783–1799. Author's Collection. (See page 89)

38D. Vase. Ht. 7½ in. *c.* 1825–1830. Author's Collection. (See page 89)

39A. Oval standing bowl. Length, 12¼ in. *c.* 1800. Author's Collection.
(See pages 61, 91, 92)

39B. Bowl on separate base. Ht. 11¼ in. Late eighteenth century. Courtesy of the
Henry Ford Museum, Dearborn (Michigan). (See pages 91, 92)

40A. Tripod bowl. Dia. 7 in. *c.* 1795. The Pilkington
Glass Museum, St. Helens. Photograph, courtesy
Howard Phillips, London. (See page 92)

40B. Bowl on silver rack. Ht. 11 in. *c.* 1790. Courtesy of the
Victoria and Albert Museum. (See page 92)

41A. Bowl with tubular stem. Ht. $7\frac{7}{8}$ in. *c*. 1800. Courtesy of the Victoria and Albert Museum. (See page 93)

41B. Bowl with stepped base. Dia. $7\frac{1}{4}$ in. *c*. 1820. Author's Collection. (See page 93)

41C. Bowl with domed base. Dia. $9\frac{1}{2}$ in. *c*. 1800. Author's Collection. (See page 93)

41D. Moulded bowl with turned-over rim. Ht. 8 in. *c*. 1800. Author's Collection. (See page 93)

41E.
Waisted bowl. Dia. $10\frac{3}{4}$ in. *c*. 1820.
Collection, The Marquess
of Bute. (See page 93)

42A.
Bowl. Ht. $5\frac{3}{10}$ in. *c*. 1820–1830. By courtesy of the National Museum of Ireland. (See page 94)

42B. Kettle drum bowl. Dia. 9 in.; Ht. $8\frac{1}{4}$ in. *c*. 1820. Author's Collection. (See page 93)

43A. Two parts of bowl shown in Plate 43B.

43B  Bowl on separate base. Dia. 10¾ in.; Ht. 8¾ in. *c.* 1825–1830. Author's Collection. (See pages 94, 130, 149)

44A. Ewer. Ht. 6¼ in. Early nineteenth century.
Collection, Down Hunt, Downpatrick.
Photograph courtesy Ulster Museum, Belfast.
(See page 95)

44B. Decanter. Ht. 6⅝ in. Early nineteenth century. Collection, Down Hunt,
Downpatrick. Photograph courtesy Ulster Museum, Belfast. (See page 95)
44C. Carafe. Ht. 6¾ in. Early nineteenth century. Collection, Down Hunt,
Downpatrick. Photograph courtesy Ulster Museum, Belfast. (See page 95)

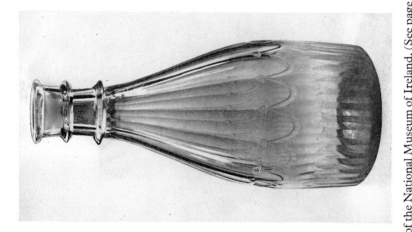

45A.  Decanter. Ht. 9 in. *c.* 1800. By courtesy of the National Museum of Ireland. (See page 95)
45B.  Decanter. Ht. 9¾ in. *c.* 1800. Ulster Museum, Belfast. (See page 95)
45C.  Decanter. Ht. 9⅝ in. *c.* 1800. Ulster Museum, Belfast. (See page 95)

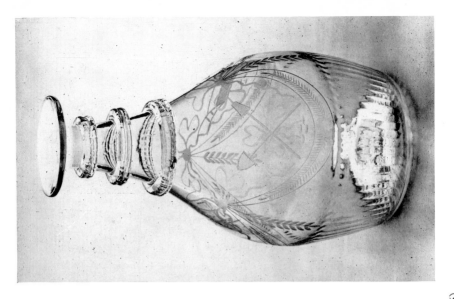

46A. Decanter. Ht. 10 in. with stopper. 1820–1850. Author's Collection. (See pages 95–96)
46B. Decanter. Ht. 9½ in. c. 1796. By courtesy of the National Museum of Ireland. (See page 96)
46C. Decanter. Ht. 8¼ in. c. 1815. By courtesy of the National Museum of Ireland. (See pages 96–97)

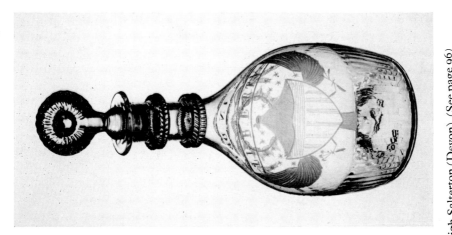

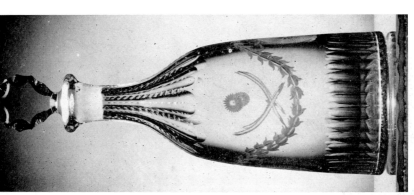

47A. Decanter. Ht. 7½ in. to lip. c. 1805. Collection, Mrs. Priscilla Hull, Budleigh Salterton (Devon). (See page 96)
47B. Decanter. Ht. 9¾ in. with stopper. c. 1800. Royal Ontario Museum/University of Toronto. (See page 96)
47C. Decanter. Ht. 8¾ in. to lip. c. 1783. Courtesy of the Victoria and Albert Museum. (See page 97)

48. Pair of decanters. Ht. to lip, 8½ in. Probably post-1783. Courtesy of the Victoria and Albert Museum. (See pages 63, 97)

FACING PAGE:

49A. (*above*) Pair of decanters. Ht. 11 in. with stoppers.
c. 1800. Collection, Mrs. Neville Fraser, Melbourne.
(See page 97)
49B. (*below*) Williamite glass: magnum decanter. Ht. 17 in.
Early nineteenth century. Ulster Museum, Belfast. (See
pages 97–98)
49C. Reverse of 49B.

50A. Decanter. Ht. 12⅞ in. with stopper. Dated 1800, possibly later. Ulster Museum, Belfast. (See page 98)

50B. Decanter. Ht. 10⅛ in. *c.* 1783–1799. Ulster Museum, Belfast. (See page 98)

51A. Decanter. Ht. 9¾ in. with stopper. *c.* 1810–1815. Author's Collection. (See pages 98–99)
51B. Decanter. Ht. 10¼ in. with stopper. *c.* 1800. The Corning Museum of Glass, Corning (New York). Ac. no. 50.2.29A. (See page 99)

52A.  Decanter. Ht. 12⅝ in. c. 1820–1830. Collection, Crawford Municipal School of Art, Cork, Barrett Bequest. (See page 99)
52B.  Two decanters. Hts. to lips, 7½ in., 7½ in. Both c. 1820–1830. Collection, Mrs. Priscilla Hull, Budleigh Salterton (Devon). (See page 99)
52C.  Decanter. Ht. 11½ in. c. 1820–1830. Collection, Crawford Municipal School of Art, Cork, Barrett Bequest. (See page 99)

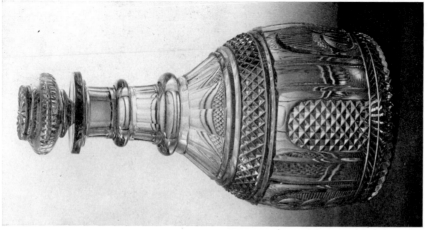

53A. Decanter. Ht. 7 in. *c.* 1825–1835. Wadsworth Atheneum, Hartford (Connecticut). The Edith Alcott van Gerbig Collection. (See page 100)

53B. Decanter. Ht. 8¾ in. *c.* 1825–1835. Ulster Museum, Belfast. (See page 100)

53C. Decanter. Ht. 9¼ in. *c.* 1825–1835. The Metropolitan Museum of Art, New York, Bequest of Annie C. Kane. (See page 100)

54A. Two jugs. Hts. 7⅞ in., 8½ in. *c.* 1815–1818. Author's Collection. (See page 100)

54B. Jug. Ht. 10 in. *c.* 1820–1830, perhaps earlier. Author's Collection. (See page 101)
54C. Jug. Ht. 8⅞ in. *c* 1820–1830, perhaps earlier. Ulster Museum, Belfast. (See page 101)

55A. Ewer. Ht. 11⅝ in. *c.* 1800–1820. Author's Collection. (See page 102)
55B. Ewer. Ht. 11½ in. *c.* 1810. Author's Collection. (See page 102)

55C. Matching ewers and decanters. Hts. 9⅞ in., 8¾ in., with stoppers. *c.* 1820–1830.
Collection, Crawford Municipal School of Art, Cork, Barrett Bequest. (See page 103)

56. Ewer. Cut and engraved. Ht. 12 in. Prior to 1800. Author's Collection.
(See page 102)

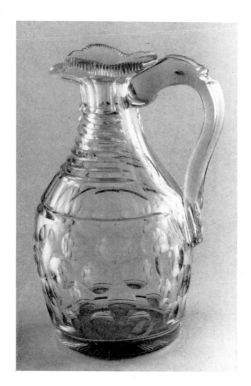

57.
Jug. Ht. 8¾ in. *c.* 1820–1830. By courtesy of the National Museum of Ireland. (See pages 86, 101)

58.
Ewer. Ht. 12⅛ in. *c.* 1783–1799. Reproduced by permission of the Syndics of the Fitzwilliam Museum, Cambridge. (See page 102)

59A. Jug. Ht. 5½ in. c. 1800. The Corning Museum of Glass, Corning (New York). Ac. no. 50.2.37. (See page 103)
59B. Jug. Ht. 5½ in. c. 1810–1815. The Corning Museum of Glass, Corning (New York). Ac. no. 51.2.219. (See page 103)

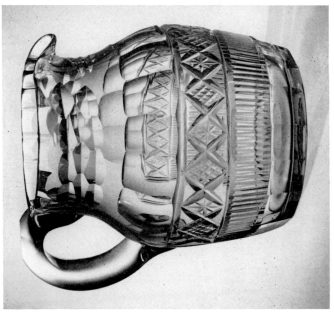

60A. Jug. Ht. 6½ in. c. 1815–1820. Author's Collection. (See page 103)
60B. Jug. Ht. 8⅞ in. c. 1820–1835. The Corning Museum of Glass, Corning (New York). Ac. no. 50.2.86. (See page 103)

61A. Salver. Dia. 6 in.; Ht. 3⅝ in. *c.* 1790. Author's Collection. (See pages 103–104)

61B. Serving dish. Length, 11¾ in. *c.* 1783–1790. Author's Collection. (See page 104)

62A.  Serving dish. Length 11½ in. *c.* 1790. Collection, Mrs. Neville Fraser, Melbourne. (See page 104)

62B.  Serving dish. Length 11¼ in. Late eighteenth century. Collection, The Marquess of Bute. (See page 104)

63A.  Serving bowl. *c.* 1783–1790. Five different lengths. Courtesy, Henry
Francis du Pont Winterthur Museum, Winterthur (Delaware).
(See page 105)

63B.  Serving bowl. Length 11⅝ in., width 9½ in. *c.* 1810–1815.
Author's Collection. (See page 105)

64A. Profile view dish Plate 64B.

64B. Octagonal dish. Dia. 9 in.; Ht. 2¼ in. *c.* 1815–1820. By courtesy of the National Museum of Ireland. (See page 105)

65A. Serving bowl. Length 10 in. Early nineteenth century.
Author's Collection. (See page 105)

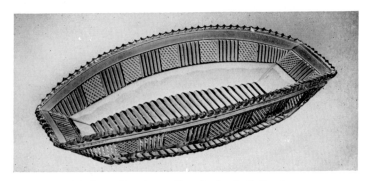

65B. Dish. Length 12 in. *c.* 1820. Author's Collection.
(See page 105)

65C. Deep circular bowl. Dia. 7½ in. *c.* 1790. Collection,
The Marquess of Bute. (See page 106)

66A. Serving bowl. Length 12½ in. *c.* 1820–1830. The Corning Museum of Glass, Corning (New York). Ac. no. 51.2.182. (See pages 105, 106)

66B. Serving bowl. Length 11½ in. *c.* 1820–1830. Collection, Crawford Municipal School of Art, Cork, Barrett Bequest. (See pages 105, 106)

66C. Square serving bowl. Dia. 9⅛ in. *c.* 1820–1830. By courtesy of the Cecil Higgins Art Gallery, Bedford. (See pages 105, 106)

67A. Round bowl. Dia. 3¾ in. *c.* 1830. Ulster Museum, Belfast.
(See page 106)

67B. Oval covered bowl. Length 10⅞ in.; Ht. 7 in. *c.* 1820. Courtesy of the Henry Ford
Museum, Dearborn (Michigan). (See pages 106, 129)

68A. (*top, left*) Butter cooler with cover. Ht. 5⅘ in.
*c.* 1783–1799. By courtesy of the Trustees of the
British Museum. (See page 106)

68B. (*top, right*) Covered jar. Ht. 6⅞ in. *c.* 1795.
Author's Collection. (See page 107)

68C. (*centre, left*) Covered jar. Ht. 7½ in. *c.* 1820–1830.
Author's Collection. (See page 107)

68D. (*left*) Covered jar. Ht. 5¾ in. *c.* 1810. Author's
Collection. (See page 107)

68E. (*above*) Covered standing jar. Ht. 6¼ in.
*c.* 1820–1830. Author's Collection.
(See page 107)

69A. Covered jar with handles. Ht. 8 in. Early nineteenth century. Ulster Museum, Belfast. (See page 108)

69B. Two covered jars, cutting unfinished on (a). Hts. 7¼ in., 7 in. c. 1825–1835. Ulster Museum, Belfast. (See page 108)

69C. Butter cooler with cover and stand. Ht. 5 in. c. 1800–1810. Author's Collection. (See page 107)

69D. Three covered jars. Ht. (a), 8¼ in. (a) and (b), after 1800; (c), before 1800. Collection, The Marquess of Bute. (See pages 107–108)

70A. Rummer. Ht. 6¼ in. Dated 1821. By courtesy of the National
Museum of Ireland. (See page 109)

70B. Goblet. Ht. 6½ in. Late eighteenth century. The Corning Museum
of Glass, Corning (New York). Ac. no. 51.2.198B. (See page 109)

70C. Goblet. Ht. 7 in. Late eighteenth – early nineteenth century. By
courtesy of the National Museum of Ireland. (See page 109)

70D. Goblet. Ht. 5 in. Late eighteenth – early nineteenth century. From
the Collection of Glasgow Art Gallery and Museum, Presented by
Thomas Fraser Campbell, 1933. (See page 109)

71A. Goblet. Ht. 4½ in. *c.* 1815. From the Collection of Glasgow Art Gallery and
Museum, The Miss J. C. C. Macdonald Bequest. (See page 109)
71B. Goblet. Ht. 4½ in. *c.* 1815. From the Collection of Glasgow Art Gallery and
Museum. The Miss J. C. C. Macdonald Bequest. (See page 109)

71C. Goblet. Ht. 5 in. Late eighteenth century. Collection, Mrs. Neville Fraser,
Melbourne. (See page 109)
71D. Goblet. Ht. 4⅜ in. Late eighteenth century. Collection, Down Hunt,
Downpatrick. Photograph courtesy Ulster Museum, Belfast. (See page 109)

72A. Stemmed glasses. Ht. (b), 5½ in. All c. 1820–1830. By courtesy of the National Museum of Ireland. (See page 109)

72B. Three tumblers. (a), c. 1820–1830; (b), 1785–1800. Probably Cork. (c), late eighteenth century. Ht. (c), 4¾ in. By courtesy of the National Museum of Ireland. (See page 109)

73A. (*top, left*) Tumbler. Ht. 4⅛ in. Early
nineteenth century. Collection,
Crawford Municipal School of Art,
Cork, Barrett Bequest. (See page 109)

73B. (*top, right*) Tumbler. Ht. 4¾ in. Early
nineteenth century. By courtesy of the
National Museum of Ireland. (See
page 110)

73C. (*centre, left*) Tumbler. Ht. 4 in.
*c.* 1783–1799. Ashmolean Museum,
Oxford, The Marshall Collection.
(See page 109)

73D. (*left*) Mug. Ht. 3⅞ in. *c.* 1820. Author's
Collection. (See pages 109–110)

73E. (*above*) Williamite glass: tumbler.
Ht. 4⅞ in. Late eighteenth – early
nineteenth century.
Collection of the Philadelphia Museum
of Art. Bequest of George H. Lorimer.
(See page 110)

74A. Four glasses in two styles. Ht. (*a*), 6 in. *c.* 1805–1830. Collection, Mrs. Priscilla Hull, Budleigh Salterton (Devon). (See pages 111–112)

74B. Three glasses and finger bowl. Ht. (*d*), 4⅜ in. Prior to 1818. Collection, Reverend R. M. L. Westropp, Windermere (Westmorland). (See page 112)

75A. Three glasses and finger bowl. Ht. (*a*), 4⅝ in. *c.* 1820–1830. Collection, The Marquess of Bute. (See page 112)

75B. Selection of sweet meat glasses. Ht. (*b*), (*c*), 4 in. Late eighteenth – early nineteenth century. (*a*)–(*d*), Author's Collection. (*e*), Collection, Mrs. John De Witt Peltz, New York. (See page 113)

75C.
Sweet meat (punch cup).
Ht. 2⅜ in.; Dia. rim, 3¼ in. Late eighteenth – early nineteenth century.
Through courtesy of the Smithsonian Institution, Washington. (See page 113)

75D.
Mixing glass. Ht. 6⅞ in.
*c.* 1785–1800.
Author's Collection.
Photograph courtesy Howard Phillips. (See page 111)

76A. Three cordial glasses. Ht. 3¾ in. *c.* 1800. Ulster Museum, Belfast. (See pages 110–111)

76B, C, D. Toasting glasses. Ht. 6 in. *c.* 1780. By courtesy of the National Museum of Ireland. (See page 110)

77A. Saucer. Dia. 4¾ in. Late eighteenth century. Author's Collection.
(See page 114)

77B. Plate. Dia. 7¾ in. *c.* 1800–1810. Author's Collection. (See pages 113–114)

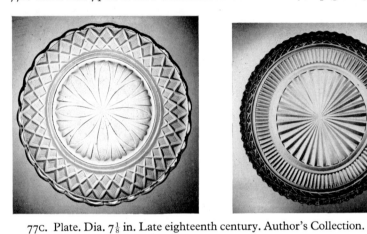

77C. Plate. Dia. 7⅛ in. Late eighteenth century. Author's Collection.
(See pages 114–115)

77D. Plate. Dia. 7 in. *c.* 1800. Collection, The Marquess of Bute.
(See pages 114–115)

77E. Plate, from the Corporation of Waterford Service. Approx.
dia. 7½ in. *c.* 1820. By permission of the Corporation of
Waterford. Gift of Senator Edward A. McGuire.
(See page 114)

78A. Two cream jugs. (*a*), Ht. 4½ in. *c.* 1810. (*b*), Ht. 3½ in.
*c.* 1800–1810. Author's Collection. (See page 115)

78B. Standing salt. Ht. 2¾ in. Late eighteenth – early nineteenth century.
Wadsworth Atheneum, Hartford (Connecticut). (See page 115)
78C. Standing salt. Ht. 2¼ in. Late eighteenth century. The Corning
Museum of Glass, Corning (New York). Ac. no. 50.2.51A.
(See page 115)

78D. Round salt. Ht. 2¼ in. *c.* 1820. Through the courtesy of the
Smithsonian Institution, Washington. (See page 116)
78E. Round salt. Ht. 2¾ in. *c.* 1820. Wadsworth Atheneum,
Hartford (Connecticut). The Edith Alcott van Gerbig
Collection. (See page 116)

79A. Piggin. Ht. 7¼ in. *c.* 1820. Courtesy of the Victoria and Albert Museum. (See page 117)
79B. Piggin. Ht. 4½ in.; dia. bowl 4⅝ in. *c.* 1820–1830. Author's Collection. (See page 117)

79C. Open salt. Dia. 4¼ in. *c.* 1830. Author's Collection. (See page 116)
79D. Octagonal saucer. Dia. 4¼ in. *c.* 1835. Author's Collection. (See page 116)

80A. Small vessels for flavourings (cruets). Ht. (*b*), 4¾ in. *c.* 1800. Author's Collection. (See page 117)

80B. Collection of sifters. Ht. (*c*) 5½ in. *c.* 1790–1830. Author's Collection. (See page 116)

81A. Miniature piggin. Ht. stave handle, 4 in.; Dia. 4¼ in. *c*. 1785–1815. By courtesy of the National Museum of Ireland. (See page 118)

81B. Miniature oval bowl. Ht. 4$\frac{9}{16}$ in. Late eighteenth century. The Corning Museum of Glass, Corning (New York). Ac. no. 50.2.43. (See page 117)

81C. Miniature oval bowl. Length 7½ in. Late eighteenth century. Collection, Mrs. Neville Fraser, Melbourne. (See page 117)

81D. Miniature jug. Ht. 4$\frac{5}{8}$ in. *c*. 1800. Collection, Mrs. Neville Fraser, Melbourne. (See page 117)

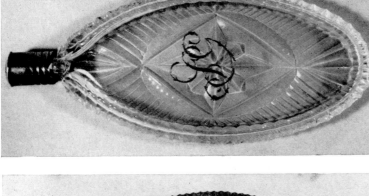

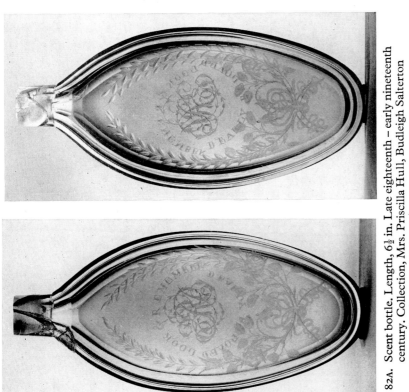

82A. Scent bottle. Length, 6½ in. Late eighteenth – early nineteenth century. Collection, Mrs. Priscilla Hull, Budleigh Salterton (Devon). (See pages 118–119)

82B. Reverse of 82A.

82C. Scent bottle. Length 5 9/10 in. Dated: 1794. By courtesy of the National Museum of Ireland. (See page 118)

82D. Scent bottle. Length 5⅖ in. c. 1790. By courtesy of the National Museum of Ireland. (See page 118)

83C. Flask. Length 6⅜ in. *c.* 1800. Courtesy of the Victoria and Albert Museum. (See page 119)

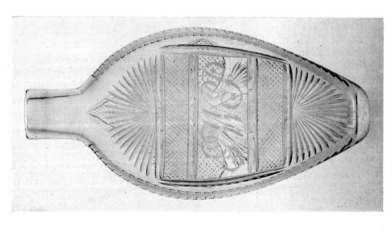

83A. Flask, Penrose initials. Length, 8 in. Late eighteenth century. Collection, Mr. Knollys Stokes, Cork. (See page 119)

83B. Reverse of 83A.

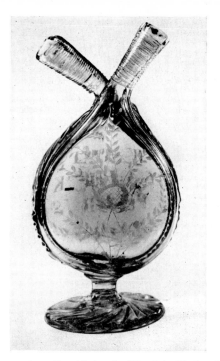

84A. Double bottle. Ht. 9¼ in. Early nineteenth century. Ulster Museum, Belfast. (See pages 119–120)

84B. Reverse of 84A.

84C. Two scent bottles; a hyacinth vase. Hts. $3\frac{3}{10}$ in., $6\frac{1}{4}$ in., $3\frac{1}{10}$ in. c. 1820–1830. By courtesy of the National Museum of Ireland. (See page 119)

85A. Hyacinth vase. Ht. 7 in. *c.* 1800–1810. Author's Collection. (See page 119)

85B. Three toddy lifters. Ht. (*b*), 7¾ in. All late eighteenth – early nineteenth century. Author's Collection. (See page 120)

85C. Linen smoother and Bowl stand. Dia. No. (*a*), 4½ in.; Ht. 5⅜ in. *c.* first half of eighteenth century. Dia. top (*b*), 5¾ in. *c.* 1770–1800. Author's Collection. (See pages 120–121)

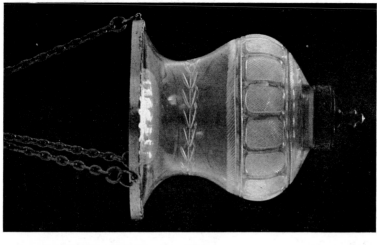

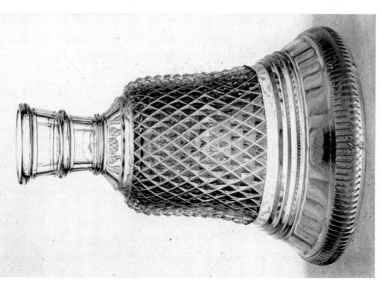

86A. (*centre*) Oval mirror. Ht. 25⅝ in.; width 16⅞ in. Late eighteenth century. Author's Collection. Ex. coll. Reverend R.M. L. Westropp. (See pages 121–122)
86B. (*left*) Hookah-base. Ht. 11 in. Early nineteenth century. Collection, Crawford Municipal School of Art, Cork. Barrett Bequest. (See page 121)
86C. (*right*) Hanging lamp. Ht. 11 in.; Dia. 9½ in. *c.* 1800–1830. Collection, Mr. Knolly Stokes, Cork. (See page 122)

87A. Ewer, two tumblers. Hts. 8¾ in., 3¾ in.

87B. Covered urn. Ht. 8¾ in.
87C. Oval bowls. Max. Length: 10¾ in.

88A. Two decanters. Max. Ht. 10¼ in.
Two wines. Max. Ht. 4⅝ in.

88B. Bowl. Length 9¼ in. Salts. 2¼ in. Plate 8 in.

89A. Covered bowl. Ht. approx. 7 in.

89B. Covered urn. Ht. approx. 13 in.

90A. Waisted bowl on stand. Dia. approx. 8¼ in.

90B. Ice pail on stand. Dia. approx. 9 in.

91A. Bowl on stand. Dia. 11½ in.

91B. Decanters on waggon. Hts. 10¾ in., 6 in.

All pieces, Collection, The Duke of Wellington, K.G.

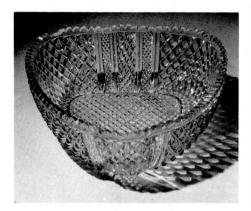

92A. Heart shaped bowl. Max. dia. 10¼ in.
92B. Leaf shaped dish. Dia. 7⅜ in.

92C. Ewer. Ht. 12½ in.

All pieces, Collection, The Duke of Wellington, K.G.

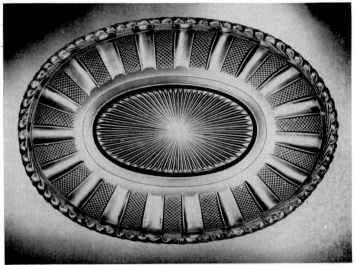

93A.
Oval bowl. Length,
$11\frac{3}{4}$ in.

93B.
Melon bowl. Ht. $6\frac{3}{4}$ in.
Jug. Ht. $6\frac{1}{2}$ in.

93C.
Circular bowl.
Dia. $11\frac{1}{2}$ in.

All pieces,
Collection,
The Marquess of Bute.

# Samuel Miller —
# Waterford Glass House Patterns

The patterns in question are drawn upon numerous separate pages, sheets and parts of sheets.[1] Thirty of these have been assembled in the nine groups which follow, Sheets 1a through 5.

Written instructions accompany many of the drawings and frequent use is made of expressions such as 'prismatic rings deep under neck'; 'starred bottoms only'; '2 rows of strawberry diamonds 3 & rings'; 'Pillars half-way up and 2 rings over and star at bottoms'; '12 strong neck flutes round . . .'

On the back of the drawing of kettle drum patterns (Sheets 4a, 5) occurs this more detailed instruction: '10-inch kettledrum, pillars and panels of X diamonds, 2 pillar rings and 3 mitred rings and fan escallop, cut bottom and stand. 12/6 each.' It will be seen that this instruction applies to the bowl identified as '4' in Sheet 5.

[1] Currently bound in Vol. 102–1927, National Museum of Ireland, reproduced here by courtesy of the Museum.

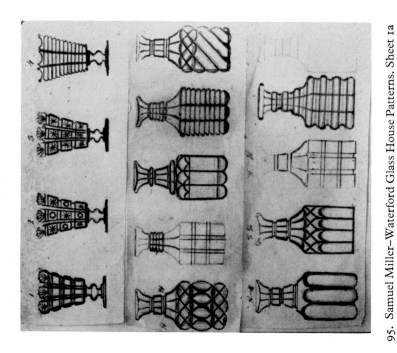

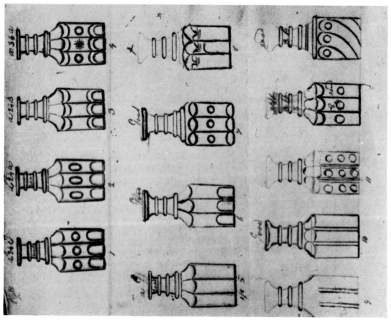

95. Samuel Miller–Waterford Glass House Patterns. Sheet 1a

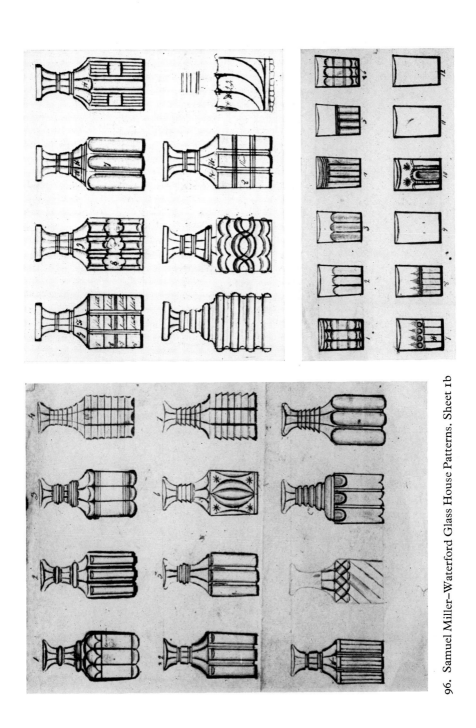

96. Samuel Miller–Waterford Glass House Patterns. Sheet 1b

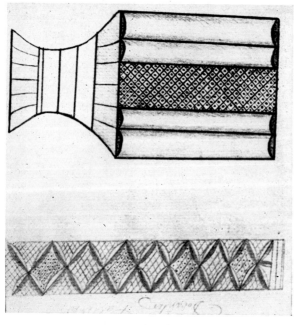

97. Samuel Miller–Waterford Glass House Patterns. Sheet 2a

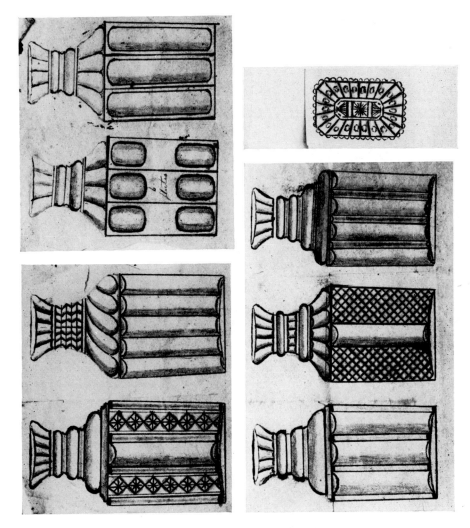

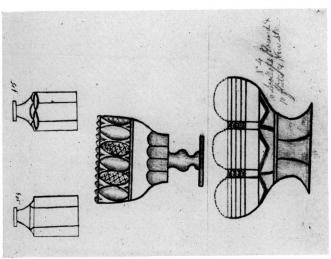

98. Samuel Miller–Waterford
Glass House Patterns. Sheet 2b

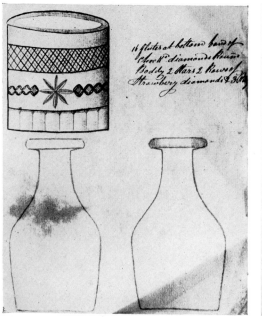

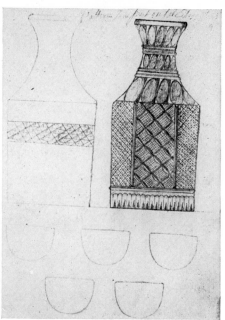

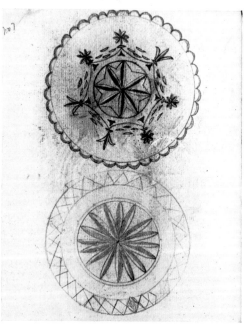

99. Samuel Miller–Waterford Glass House Patterns. Sheet 3a

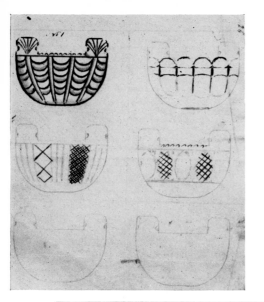
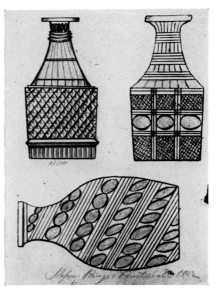
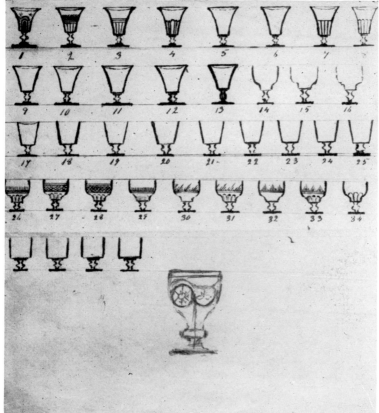

100. Samuel Miller–Waterford Glass House Patterns. Sheet 3b

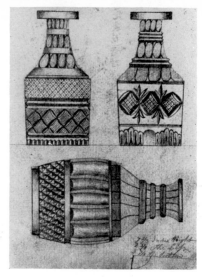
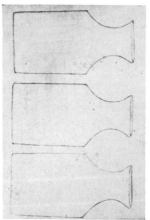
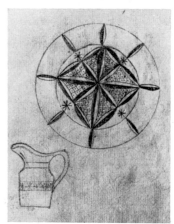
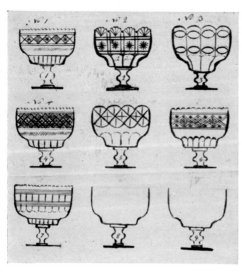
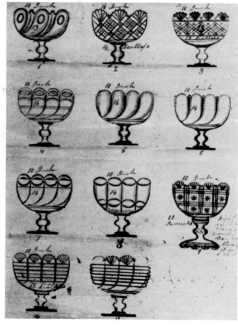

101. Samuel Miller–Waterford
Glass House Patterns. Sheet 4a

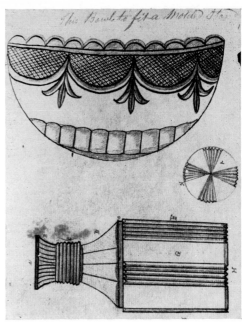

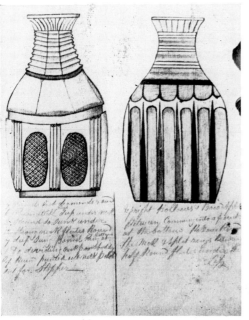

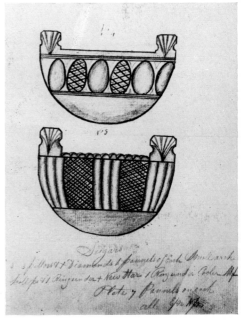

102. Samuel Miller–Waterford Glass House Patterns. Sheet 4b

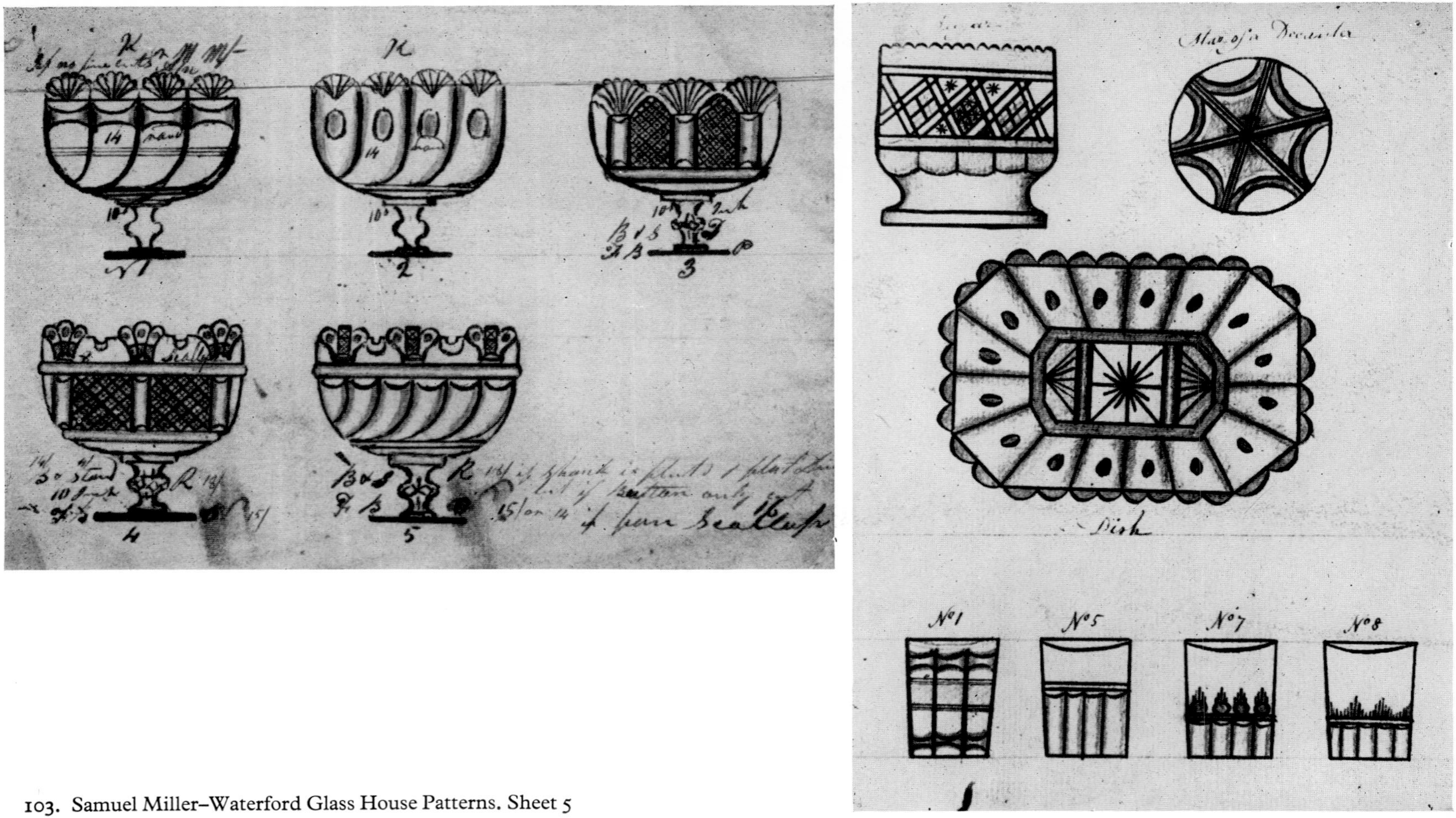


103. Samuel Miller–Waterford Glass House Patterns. Sheet 5